Traditional Catholic Prayers in Latin and English

With additional Devotions for Mass, Litanies, and Psalms

CATHOLIC DEVOTIONS

First Edition 2021
Revised, April 2022

Contents

PART I - ENGLISH AND LATIN
COMMON PRAYERS

PART II - ENGLISH:
DEVOTIONS FOR MASS; LITANIES; PSALMS

Prayers of the Rosary

Listed in English and Latin
by order of their recitation.

This page intentionally blank.

How to Pray the Rosary

1. Begin with the Sign of the Cross.
2. Say the Apostles' Creed.
3. On the first bead, say an Our Father.
4. On the three following beads, say a Hail Mary for the theological virtues of Faith, Hope, and Charity.
5. Say the Glory Be.
6. For each of the five decades, announce the Mystery (optional: a brief reading from Scripture) then say the Our Father.
7. On each of the ten beads of the decade, say the Hail Mary while meditating on the Mystery. Finish with a Glory Be (after finishing each decade, you may say the "Fatima Prayer" requested by the Blessed Virgin Mary at Fatima).
8. After saying the five decades, say the Hail, Holy Queen, followed by the concluding prayer.
9. Optional: Many say the St. Michael Prayer after finishing the rosary.

The Mysteries

Joyful

(Mondays/Saturdays/Sundays of Advent)

Annunciation: Luke 1:26-27

Visitation: Luke 1:39-42

Nativity: Luke 2:1-7

Presentation: Luke 2:21-24

Finding of Jesus in the Temple: Luke 2:41-47

Sorrowful

(Tuesdays/Fridays/Sundays of Lent)

Agony in the Garden: Matthew 26:36-39

Scourging at the Pillar: Matthew 27:26

Crowning with Thorns: Matthew 27:27-29

Carrying of the Cross: Mark 15:21-22

Crucifixion: Luke 23:33-46

Glorious

(Wednesdays/Sundays)

Resurrection: Luke 24:1-5

Ascension: Mark 16:19

Descent of the Holy Spirit: Acts 2:1-4

Assumption: Luke 1:48-49

Coronation: Revelation 12:1

Luminous

(Thursdays)

Baptism of Christ: Matthew 3:16-17

Wedding Feast at Cana: John 2:1-5

Proclamation of the Kingdom: Mark 1:15

Transfiguration: Matthew 17:1-2

Institution of the Eucharist: Matthew 26:26

Sign of the Cross

In the name of the Father, and of the Son, and of the
Holy Spirit.
Amen.

Apostles' Creed

I believe in God, the Father almighty, Creator of
heaven and earth, and in Jesus Christ, His only Son,
our Lord, Who was conceived by the power of the
Holy Spirit and born of the Virgin Mary, suffered
under Pontius Pilate, was crucified, died, and was
buried; He descended into hell; on the third day He
rose again from the dead; He ascended into heaven and
is seated at the right hand of God, the Father
Almighty; from there He will come to judge the living
and the dead. I believe in the Holy Spirit, the holy
catholic Church, the communion of saints, the
forgiveness of sins, the resurrection of the body, and
the life everlasting.
Amen.

Signum Crucis

In nomine Patris, et Filii, et Spiritus Sancti.
Amen.

Symbolum Apostolorum

Credo in Deum Patrem omnipotentem, Creatorem
caeli et terrae. Et in Iesum Christum, Filium eius
unicum, Dominum nostrum, qui conceptus est de
Spiritu Sancto, natus ex Maria Virgine, passus sub
Pontio Pilato, crucifixus, mortuus, et sepultus,
descendit ad inferos, tertia die resurrexit a mortuis,
ascendit ad caelos, sedet ad dexteram Dei Patris
omnipotentis, inde venturus est iudicare vivos et
mortuos. Credo in Spiritum Sanctum, sanctam
Ecclesiam catholicam, sanctorum communionem,
remissionem peccatorum, carnis resurrectionem,
vitam aeternam.
Amen.

The Lord's Prayer (Our Father)

Our Father, who art in heaven, hallowed be Thy name.
Thy kingdom come. Thy will be done on earth as it is
in heaven. Give us this day our daily bread and forgive
us our trespasses as we forgive those who trespass
against us. And lead us not into temptation, but
deliver us from evil.
Amen.

Hail Mary

Hail Mary, full of grace, the Lord is with thee. Blessed
art thou amongst women and blessed is the fruit of thy
womb, Jesus. Holy Mary, Mother of God, pray for us
sinners, now, and in the hour of our death.
Amen.

Oratio Dominica (Pater Noster)

Pater Noster, qui es in caelis, sanctificetur nomen tuum. Adveniat regnum tuum. Fiat voluntas tua, sicut in caelo et in terra. Panem nostrum quotidianum da nobis hodie, et dimitte nobis debita nostra sicut et nos dimittimus debitoribus nostris. Et ne nos inducas in tentationem, sed libera nos a malo.
Amen.

Ave Maria

Ave Maria, gratia plena, Dominus tecum. Benedicta tu in mulieribus, et benedictus fructus ventris tui, Iesus. Sancta Maria, Mater Dei, ora pro nobis peccatoribus, nunc, et in hora mortis nostrae.
Amen.

Doxology (Glory Be)

Glory be to the Father, and to the Son, and to the
Holy Spirit. As it was in the beginning, is now, and
will be forever.
Amen.

Fatima Prayer

O my Jesus, forgive us our sins, save us from the fires
of hell, and lead all souls to heaven, especially those
most in need of Thy mercy.
Amen.

Gloria Patri

Gloria Patri, et Filio, et Spiritui Sancto. * Sicut erat in principio, et nunc, et semper, et in saecula saeculorum. Amen.

Oratio Fatima

Domine Iesu, dimitte nobis debita nostra, salva nos ab igne inferiori, perduc in caelum omnes animas, praesertim eas quae misericordiae tuae maximae indigent.
Amen.

Hail, Holy Queen

Hail, holy Queen, Mother of mercy, our life, our sweetness and our hope. To thee do we cry, poor banished children of Eve. To thee to we send up our sighs, mourning and weeping in this valley of tears. Turn, then, most gracious advocate, thine eyes of mercy toward us, and after this, our exile, show unto us the blessed fruit of thy womb, Jesus. O clement, O loving, O sweet Virgin Mary.

V. Pray for us, O holy Mother of God.

R. That we may be made worthy of the promises of Christ.

Amen.

Salve, Regina

Salve, Regina, mater misericordiae; vita, dulcedo et spes nostra, salve. Ad te clamamus exsules filii Hevae. Ad te suspiramus gementes et flentes in hac lacrimarum valle. Eia ergo, advocata nostra, illos tuos misericordes oculos ad nos converte. Et Iesum, benedictum fructum ventris tui, nobis post hoc exsilium ostende. O clemens, o pia, o dulcis Virgo Maria.

V. Ora pro nobis, sancta Dei Genitrix.
R. Ut digni efficamur promissionibus Christi. Amen.

O God, Whose Only-Begotten Son

(this prayer is often added after the Hail Holy Queen)

Let us pray. O God, Whose Only-Begotten Son, by His life, death and resurrection, has purchased for us the rewards of eternal life: grant, we beseech Thee, that by meditating upon these mysteries of the most holy Rosary of the Blessed Virgin Mary, we may imitate what they contain, and obtain what they promise, through the same Christ our Lord.
Amen.

Post Salve, Regina

Deus, cuius Unigenitus per vitam, mortem et resurrectionem suam nobis salutis aeternae praemia comparavit: concede, quaesumus; ut, haec mysteria sacratissimo beatae Mariae Virginis Rosario recolentes. et imitemur quod continent, et quod promittunt, assequamur. Per eundem Christum Dominum nostrum.
Amen.

Prayer to St. Michael

Saint Michael the Archangel, defend us in battle; be our defense against the wickedness and snares of the devil. May God rebuke him, we humbly pray. And do thou, O prince of the heavenly host, by the power of God thrust into hell Satan and all the evil spirits who prowl about the world for the ruin of souls.
Amen.

Oratio ad Sanctum Michael

Sancte Michael Archangele, defende nos in proelio, contra nequitiam et insidias diaboli esto praesidium. Imperet illi Deus, supplices deprecamur: tuque, Princeps militiae caelestis, Satanam aliosque spiritus malignos, qui ad perditionem animarum pervagantur in mundo, divina virtute, in infernum detrude.
Amen.

This page intentionally blank.

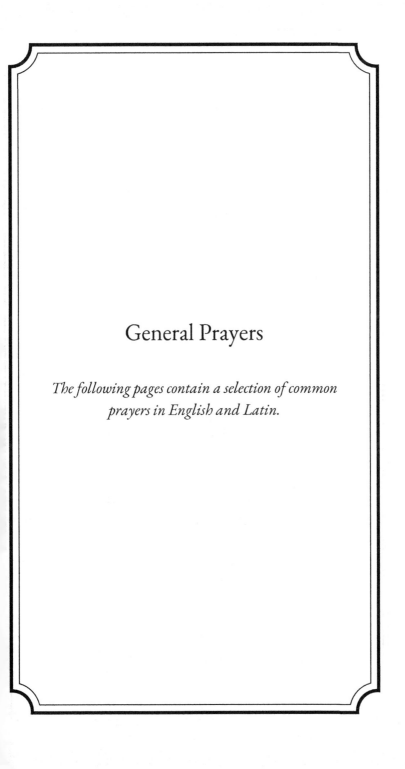

General Prayers

The following pages contain a selection of common prayers in English and Latin.

Blessing Before Meals

Bless us, O Lord, and these Thy gifts which we are about to receive from Thy bounty, through Christ our Lord. Amen.

Blessing After Meals

We give Thee thanks, almighty God, for all Thy benefits, who lives and reigns for ever and ever. Amen.

V. May the Lord grant us His peace.
R. And life everlasting.
Amen.

Benedictio Ante Mensam

Benedic, Domine, nos et haec tua dona quae de tua largitate sumus sumpturi. Per Christum Dominum nostrum. Amen.

Benedictio Post Mensam

Agimus tibi gratias, omnipotens Deus, pro universis beneficiis tuis, qui vivis et regnas in saecula saeculorum. Amen.

V. Deus det nobis suam pacem.
R. Et vitam aeternam.
Amen.

Morning Prayer

Psalm 62 (63) - taken from Lauds in the Liturgy of the Hours

V. O God, come to my assistance.
R. O Lord, make haste to help me.
Glory be...

Antiphon: For thee at dawn will I watch O God, that I may behold thy glory and power

O God, my God, to thee do I watch at break of day. For thee my soul hath thirsted; for thee my flesh, O how many ways! In a desert land, and where there is no way, and no water: so in the sanctuary have I come before thee, to see thy power and thy glory. For thy mercy is better than lives: thee my lips shall praise. Thus will I bless thee all my life long: and in thy name I will lift up my hands.
Let my soul be filled as with marrow and fatness: and my mouth shall praise thee with joyful lips. If I have remembered thee upon my bed, I will meditate on thee in the morning: Because thou hast been my helper. And I will rejoice under the covert of thy wings: My soul hath stuck close to thee: thy right hand hath received me. But they have sought my soul in vain, they shall go into the lower parts of the earth:
They shall be delivered into the hands of the sword, they shall be the portions of foxes. But the king shall rejoice in God, all they shall be praised that swear by him: because the mouth is stopped of them that speak wicked things.

Glory be...
Antiphon.

Morning Prayer

V. Deus in adjutorium meum intende.
R. Domine ad adjuvandum me festina.
Gloria Patri, et Filio, et Spiritui Sancto...

Antiphon: Ad te de luce vigilo Deus, ut videam virtutem tuam.

Deus, Deus meus, ad te de luce vigilo. Sitivit in te anima mea; quam multipliciter tibi caro mea!
In terra deserta, et invia, et inaquosa, sic in sancto apparui tibi, ut viderem virtutem tuam et gloriam tuam.
Quoniam melior est misericordia tua super vitas, labia mea laudabunt te.
Sic benedicam te in vita mea, et in nomine tuo levabo manus meas.
Sicut adipe et pinguedine repleatur anima mea, et labiis exsultationis laudabit os meum.
Si memor fui tui super stratum meum, in matutinis meditabor in te.
Quia fuisti adjutor meus, et in velamento alarum tuarum exsultabo.
Adhæsit anima mea post te; me suscepit dextera tua.
Ipsi vero in vanum quæsierunt animam meam: introibunt in inferiora terræ;
tradentur in manus gladii: partes vulpium erunt.
Rex vero lætabitur in Deo; laudabuntur omnes qui jurant in eo: quia obstructum est os loquentium iniqua.Amen.

Gloria Patri, et Filio, et Spiritui Sancto...
Antiphon.

Evening Prayer

(taken from Luke 2:29-32)

Now let thy servant depart in peace, O Lord,
According to thy word;
For mine eyes have seen thy salvation,
Which thou hast prepared before the face of all peoples;
A light for revelation to the Gentiles,
And the glory of thy people Israel.
Amen.

Nunc Dimittis

Nunc dimittis servum tuum Domine,
secundum verbum tuum in pace:
quia viderunt oculi mei salutare tuum,
quod parasti ante faciem omnium populorum:
lumen ad revelationem gentium,
et gloriam plebis tuæ Israel.
Amen.

Angel of God

Angel of God,
my guardian dear,
To whom his love commits me here;
Ever this [day / night] be at my side,
To light and guard, to rule and guide.
Amen.

Angele Dei

Angele Dei, qui custos es mei,
Me tibi commissum pietate superna;
[Hodie / Hac nocte] illumina, custodi, rege, et guberna.
Amen.

Act of Faith

O Lord God, I firmly believe each and every truth which the holy Catholic Church teaches, because Thou, O God, Who are eternal truth and wisdom which can neither deceive nor be deceived, hast revealed them all. In this faith I stand to live and die. Amen.

Act of Hope

O Lord God, through Thy grace I hope to obtain remission of all my sins and after this life eternal happiness, for Thou hast promised, Who are all powerful, faithful, kind, and merciful. In this hope I stand to live and die. Amen.

Act of Love

O Lord God, I love Thee above all things, and I love my neighbor on account of Thee, because Thou are the highest, infinite and most perfect good, worthy of all love. In this love I stand to live and die. Amen.

Actus Fidei

Domine Deus, firma fide credo et confiteor omnia et singula quae sancta ecclesia Catholica proponit, quia tu, Deus, ea omnia revelasti, qui es aeterna veritas et sapientia quae nec fallere nec falli potest. In hac fide vivere et mori statuo. Amen.

Actus Spei

Domine Deus, spero per gratiam tuam remissionem omnium peccatorum, et post hanc vitam aeternam felicitatem me esse consecuturum: quia tu promisisti, qui es infinite potens, fidelis, benignus, et misericors. In hac spe vivere et mori statuo. Amen.

Actus Caritatis

Domine Deus, amo te super omnia et proximum meum propter te, quia tu es summum, infinitum, et perfectissimum bonum, omni dilectione dignum. In hac caritate vivere et mori statuo. Amen.

De Profundis

Out of the depths have I cried unto thee, O Lord :
Lord, hear my voice.

Oh, let thine ears consider well : the voice of my
supplication.

If thou, O Lord, shalt mark iniquities : Lord who shall
abide it ?

For with thee there is propitiation : and because of thy
law I have waited for thee, O Lord.

My soul hath waited on his word: my soul hath hoped
in the Lord.

From the morning watch even until night : let Israel
hope in the Lord.

For with the Lord there is mercy: and with him
plenteous redemption.

And he shall redeem Israel: from all his iniquities.

Eternal rest give unto them, O Lord.
And let perpetual light shine up on them.
May they rest in peace.
Amen.

De Profundis

De profundis clamavi ad te, Domine:
Domine, exaudi vocem meam:
Fiant aures tuae intendentes,
in vocem deprecationis meae.
Si iniquitates observaveris, Domine:
Domine, quis sustinebit?
Quia apud te propitiatio est:
et propter legem tuam sustinui te, Domine.
Sustinuit anima mea in verbo eius:
speravit anima mea in Domino.
A custodia matutina usque ad noctem:
speret Israel in Domino.
Quia apud Dominum misericordia:
et copiosa apud eum redemptio.
Et ipse redimet Israel,
ex omnibus iniquitatibus eius.

Requiem æternam dona eis, Domine.
Et lux perpetua luceat eis.
Requiescant in pace.
Amen.

This page intentionally blank.

Marian Prayers

*Prayers in English and Latin to the Blessed Virgin Mary,
in alphabetical order by the Latin titles.*

Alma Redemptoris Mater

Mother of Christ, hear thou thy people's cry. Star of the deep and Portal of the sky! Mother of Him who thee made from nothing made. Sinking we strive and call to thee for aid: Oh, by what joy which Gabriel brought to thee, thou Virgin first and last, let us thy mercy see.

During Advent
V. The Angel of the Lord announced unto Mary.
R. And she conceived by the Holy Ghost.

Let us pray:
Pour forth, we beseech Thee, O Lord, Thy grace into our hearts: that as we have known the incarnation of Thy Son Jesus Christ by the message of an Angel, so too by His Cross and passion may we be brought to the glory of His resurrection.
Amen.

From Christmas Eve until the Purification
V. After childbirth thou didst remain a virgin.
R. Intercede for us, O Mother of God.

Let us pray:
O God, who, by the fruitful virginity of blessed Mary, hast bestowed upon mankind the reward of eternal salvation: grant, we beseech Thee, that we may experience her intercession, through whom we have been made worthy to receive the author of life, our Lord Jesus Christ, Thy Son.
Amen.

Alma Redemptoris Mater

Alma Redemptoris Mater, quae pervia caeli
Porta manes, et stella maris, succurre cadenti, Surgere qui curat,
populo: tu quae genuisti, Natura mirante, tuum sanctum Genitorem
Virgo prius ac posterius, Gabrielis ab ore Sumens illud Ave,
peccatorum miserere.

Tempus Adventus [During Advent]
V. Angelus Domini nuntiavit Mariae.
R. Et concepit de Spiritu Sancto.

Oremus:
Gratiam tuam, quaesumus, Domine, mentibus nostris infunde: ut
qui, Angelo nuntiante, Christi Filii tui incarnationem cognovimus;
per passionem eius et crucem, ad resurrectionis gloriam perducamur.
Per eundem Christum Dominum nostrum.
Amen.

Donec Purificatio [Christmas Eve until the Purification]
V. Post partum, Virgo, inviolata permansisti.
R. Dei Genetrix, intercede pro nobis.

Oremus:
Deus, qui salutis aeternae, beatae Mariae virginitate fecunda,
humano generi praemia praestitisti: tribue, quaesumus; ut ipsam pro
nobis intercedere sentiamus, per quam meruimus auctorem vitae
suscipere, Dominum nostrum Iesum Christum, Filium tuum.
Amen.

Hail Star of the Sea

Hail, O Star of the sea,
God's own Mother blest,
ever sinless Virgin,
gate of heavenly rest.

Taking that sweet Ave,
which from Gabriel came,
peace confirm within us,
changing Eve's name.

Break the sinners' fetters,
make our blindness day,
Chase all evils from us,
for all blessings pray.

Show thyself a Mother,
may the Word divine
born for us thine Infant
hear our prayers through thine.

Virgin all excelling,
mildest of the mild,
free from guilt preserve us
meek and undefiled.

Keep our life all spotless,
make our way secure
till we find in Jesus,
joy for evermore.

Praise to God the Father,
honor to the Son,
in the Holy Spirit,
be the glory one.
Amen.

Ave Maris Stella

Ave maris stella,
Dei Mater alma,
atque semper Virgo,
felix caeli porta.

Sumens illud Ave
Gabrielis ore,
funda nos in pace,
mutans Hevae nomen.

Solve vincula reis,
profer lumen caecis
mala nostra pelle,
bona cuncta posce.

Monstra te esse matrem:
sumat per te preces,
qui pro nobis natus,
tulit esse tuus.

Virgo singularis,
inter omnes mites,
nos culpis solutos,
mitis fac et castos.

Vitam praesta puram,
iter para tutum:
ut videntes Iesum
semper collaetemur.

Sit laus Deo Patri,
summo Christo decus,
Spiritui Sancto,
tribus honor unus.
Amen.

Ave Regina Caelorum

Hail, O Queen of Heaven enthroned!
Hail, by angels Mistress owned
Root of Jesse, Gate of morn,
Whence the world's true Light was born.

Glorious Virgin, joy to thee,
Loveliest whom in Heaven they see:
Fairest thou where all are fair,
Plead with Christ our sins to spare.

V. Allow me to praise thee, O holy Virgin.
R. Give me strength against thy enemies.

Grant, O merciful God, to our weak natures Thy protection,
that we who commemorate the holy Mother of God may, by
the help of her intercession, arise from our iniquities.
Through the same Christ our Lord.
Amen.

Ave Regina Caelorum

Ave, Regina caelorum,
Ave, Domina Angelorum:
Salve, radix, salve, porta
Ex qua mundo lux est orta:

Gaude, Virgo gloriosa,
Super omnes speciosa,
Vale, o valde decora,
Et pro nobis Christum exora.

V. Dignare me laudare te, Virgo sacrata.
R. Da mihi virtutem contra hostes tuos.

Oremus. Concede, misericors Deus, fragilitati nostrae
praesidium: ut, qui sanctae Dei Genitricis memoriam agimus;
intercessionis eius auxilio, a nostris iniquitatibus resurgamus.
Per eundem Christum Dominum nostrum.
Amen.

The Angelus

V. The angel of the Lord declared unto Mary.
R. And she conceived of the Holy Spirit.

Hail Mary, full of grace; the Lord is with Thee: blessed art thou among women, and blessed is the fruit of thy womb, Jesus. Holy Mary, Mother of God, prayer for us sinners, now and at the hour of our death.

V. Behold the handmaid of the Lord,
R. Be it done to me according to Thy word.
Hail Mary...

V. And the Word was made flesh,
R. And dwelt among us.
Hail Mary...

V. Pray for us, O holy Mother of God,
R. That we may be made worthy of the promises of Christ.

Let us pray:
Pour forth, we beseech Thee, Lord, Thy grace into our hearts; that, as we have known the Incarnation of Christ, Thy Son, by the message of an angel, so by His Passion and Cross we may be brought to the glory of the Resurrection. Through the same Christ our Lord.
Amen.

The Angelus is traditionally recited three times a day, usually at 9, noon, and 6.

Angelus

V. Angelus Domini nuntiavit Mariae.
R. Et concepit de Spiritu Sancto.

Ave Maria, gratia plena; Dominus tecum: benedicta tu in mulieribus, et benedictus fructus ventris tui Iesus. Sancta Maria, Mater Dei ora pro nobis peccatoribus, nunc et in hora mortis nostrae.

V. Ecce ancilla Domini,
R. Fiat mihi secundum verbum tuum.

Ave Maria ...

V. Et Verbum caro factum est,
R. Et habitavit in nobis.

Ave Maria ...

V. Ora pro nobis, sancta Dei Genetrix,
R. Ut digni efficiamur promissionibus Christi.

Oremus:
Gratiam tuam, quaesumus, Domine, mentibus nostris infunde; ut qui, Angelo nuntiante, Christi Filii tui incarnationem cognovimus, per passionem eius et crucem ad resurrectionis gloriam perducamur. Per eumdem Christum Dominum nostrum. Amen.

IN comm after the Angelus —
Pray Regina Coeli Po39

Inviolate Mary

Inviolate, spotless and pure art thou,
O Mary Who was made the radiant gate of the King.
Holy mother of Christ most dear,
receive our devout hymn and praise.
Our hearts and tongues now ask of thee
that our souls and bodies may be pure.
By thy sweet sounding prayers
obtain for us forgiveness forever.
O gracious queen, O Mary,
who alone among women art inviolate.
Amen.

Inviolata

Inviolata, integra, et casta es Maria,
quae es effecta fulgida caeli porta.
O Mater alma Christi carissima,
suscipe pia laudum praeconia.
Te nunc flagitant devota corda et ora,
nostra ut pura pectora sint et corpora.
Tu per precata dulcisona,
nobis concedas veniam per saecula.
O benigna! O Regina! O Maria,
quae sola inviolata permansisti.
Amen.

The Memorare

Remember, O most gracious Virgin Mary, that never was it known that anyone who fled to thy protection, implored thy help, or sought thy intercession was left unaided. Inspired with this confidence, I fly to thee, O Virgin of virgins, my Mother; to thee do I come; before thee I stand, sinful and sorrowful. O Mother of the Word Incarnate, despise not my petitions, but in thy mercy hear and answer me.

Amen.

Memorare, O piisima Virgo Maria

Memorare, O piissima Virgo Maria, non esse auditum a saeculo, quemquam ad tua currentem praesidia, tua implorantem auxilia, tua petentem suffragia, esse derelictum. Ego tali animatus confidentia, ad te, Virgo Virginum, Mater, curro, ad te venio, coram te gemens peccator assisto. Noli, Mater Verbi, verba mea despicere; sed audi propitia et exaudi.

Amen.

Magnificat

And Mary said: My soul magnifies the Lord.

And my spirit rejoices in God my Savior.

Because he has regarded the humility of his handmaid; for behold from henceforth all generations shall call me blessed.

Because he that is mighty, has done great things to me; and holy is his name.

And his mercy is from generation unto generations, to them that fear him.

He has shown might in his arm: he has scattered the proud in the conceit of their heart.

He has put down the mighty from their seat, and has exalted the humble.

He has filled the hungry with good things; and the rich he has sent empty away.

He has received Israel his servant, being mindful of his mercy:

As he spoke to our fathers, to Abraham and to his seed for ever.

Amen.

Magnificat

Magnificat anima mea Dominum, et exultavit spiritus meus in Deo salvatore meo, quia respexit humilitatem ancillae suae.

Ecce enim ex hoc beatam me dicent omnes generationes, quia fecit mihi magna, qui potens est, et sanctum Nomen eius, et misericordia eius in progenies et progenies timentibus eum.

Fecit potentiam in brachio suo, dispersit superbos mente cordi sui; deposuit potentes de sede et exaltavit humiles; esurientes implevit bonis et divites dimisit inanes.

Suscepit Israel puerum suum, recordatus misericordiae, sicut locutus est ad patres nostros, Abraham et semini eius in saecula.

Amen.

Queen of Heaven

O Queen of heaven rejoice! alleluia:
For He whom thou didst merit to bear, alleluia,
Hath arisen as he said, alleluia.
Pray for us to God, alleluia.
Rejoice and be glad, O Virgin Mary, alleluia.
Because the Lord is truly risen, alleluia.

O God, who gave joy to the world through the resurrection of Thy Son, our Lord Jesus Christ, grant we beseech Thee, that through the intercession of the Virgin Mary, His Mother, we may obtain the joys of everlasting life. Through the same Christ our Lord. Amen.

Regina Caeli

Regina, caeli, laetare, alleluia:
Quia quem meruisti portare, alleluia,
Resurrexit sicut dixit, alleluia.
Ora pro nobis Deum, alleluia.
Gaude et laetare, Virgo Maria, alleluia,
Quia surrexit Dominus vere, alleluia.

Deus, qui per resurrectionem Filii tui, Domini nostri
Iesu Christi, mundum laetificare dignatus es: praesta,
quaesumus; ut per eius Genetricem Virginem Mariam,
perpetuae capiamus gaudia vitae. Per eundem
Christum Dominum nostrum.
Amen

Hail Holy Queen

Hail Holy Queen, Mother of mercy, our life, our sweetness, and our hope. To thee do we cry, poor banished children of Eve. To thee do we send up our sighs, mourning and weeping in this valley of tears. Turn then, most gracious Advocate, thine eyes of mercy toward us. And after this our exile show unto us the blessed fruit of thy womb, Jesus.
O clement, O loving, O sweet Virgin Mary.

V. Pray for us, O Holy Mother of God.
R. That we may be made worthy of the promises of Christ.
Amen

Salve Regina

Salve, Regina, mater misericordiae, vita, dulcedo, et
spes nostra, salve. Ad te clamamus exsules filii Hevae.
Ad te suspiramus, gementes et flentes in hac
lacrimarum valle.
Eia, ergo, advocata nostra, illos tuos misericordes
oculos ad nos converte. Et Iesum, benedictum
fructum ventris tui, nobis post hoc exsilium ostende.
O clemens, O pia, O dulcis Virgo Maria.

V. Ora pro nobis, sancta Dei Genetrix.
R. Ut digni efficiamur promissionibus Christi.
Amen.

Under thy Patronage

We fly to thy patronage, O holy Mother of God; despise
not our petitions in our necessities, but deliver us always
from all dangers, O glorious and blessed Virgin.
Amen.

Sub tuum Praesidium

Sub tuum praesidium confugimus, Sancta Dei Genetrix.
Nostras deprecationes ne despicias in necessitatibus, sed
a periculis cunctis libera nos semper, Virgo gloriosa et
benedicta.
Amen.

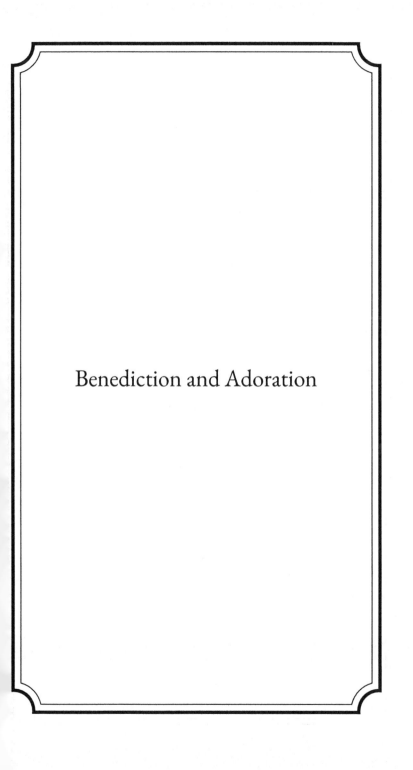

Benediction and Adoration

The order of Exposition / Benediction

1.) Stand: The presider enters the chapel with the Host; a song may be sung.

2.) Kneel: While the presider places the Host into the monstrance.

3.) The presider will lead all in singing an appropriate Eucharistic song, typically O Saving Victim/ O Salutaris.

4.) Stand or be Seated: After incensing the monstrance, the presider will instruct all to stand (for a Gospel reading) or be seated (for another scripture reading) followed by a short reflection.

Adoration

5.) Kneel or be Seated: After the reading(s) and reflection are completed, the private portion of adoration/devotion begins.

Benediction

6.) Kneel: Once private adoration/devotion is completed, the presider will incense the monstrance. All sing an appropriate Eucharistic song, typically Tantum Ergo.

7.) All remain kneeling as the presider leads in a prayer.

8.) Continue kneeling for the elevation of the monstrance and the recitation of the Divine Praises.

9.) Stand for Reposition of the Blessed Sacrament, singing an appropriate hymn - typically Holy God We Praise Thy Name.*

This section contains the main hymns/prayers said before the Blessed Sacrament, in the order they appear during exposition / adoration / benediction. There are four additional hymns/prayers suitable for recitation.

*Not included in the English/Latin as the original is a German hymn. However, it is based on the Te Deum Laudamus, which can be found below.

O Saving Victim

O Saving Victim opening wide
The gate of heaven to man below
Our foes press on from every side;
Thine aid supply, thy strength bestow.

To thy great name be endless praise,
Immortal Godhead , one in three !
Oh, grant us endless length of days
In our true native land with thee !
Amen.

O Salutaris Hostia

O Salutaris Hostia
Quae caeli pandis ostium.
Bella premunt hostilia;
Da robur, fer auxilium.

Uni trinoque Domino
Sit sempiterna gloria:
Qui vitam sine termino,
Nobis donet in patria.
Amen.

Sing, my tongue, the glory / Down in Adoration Falling

Sing, my tongue, the Savior's glory
Of his flesh the mystery sing;
Of the Blood, all price exceeding,
Shed by our immortal King,
Destined for the world's redemption,
From a noble womb to spring.

Of a pure and spotless Virgin
Born for us on earth below,
He, as man with man conversing,
Stayed, the seeds of truth to sow;
Then he closed in solemn order
Wondrously his life of woe.

On the night of that Last supper,
Seated with his chosen band,
He the paschal victim eating,
First fulfils the law's command;
Then, as food to all his brethren,
Gives himself with his own hand.

Word made flesh, the bread of nature
By his word to flesh he turns:
Wine into his blood he changes:
What though sense no change
discerns?

Pange, lingua, gloriosi / Tantum Ergo

Pange, lingua, gloriosi
Corporis mysterium,
Sanguinisque pretiosi,
quem in mundi pretium
fructus ventris generosi
Rex effudit Gentium.

Nobis datus, nobis natus
ex intacta Virgine,
et in mundo conversatus,
sparso verbi semine,
sui moras incolatus
miro clausit ordine.

In supremae nocte cenae
recumbens cum fratribus
observata lege plene
cibis in legalibus,
cibum turbae duodenae
se dat suis manibus.

Verbum caro, panem verum
verbo carnem efficit:
fitque sanguis Christi merum,
et si sensus deficit,
ad firmandum cor sincerum
sola fides sufficit.

Down in adoration falling,
Lo! the sacred host we hail;
Lo! o'er ancient forms departing,
Newer rites of grace prevail!
Faith, for all defects supplying,
Where the feeble senses fail.

To the everlasting Father,
And the Son who reigns on high,
With the Holy Ghost proceeding,
Forth from each eternally,
Be salvation, honor, blessing,
Might, and endless majesty.

V. Thou didst give them bread
from heaven. [Alleluia.]
R. Containing in itself all
sweetness. [Alleluia.]

Tantum ergo Sacramentum
veneremur cernui:
et antiquum documentum
novo cedat ritui:
praestet fides supplementum
sensuum defectui.

Genitori, Genitoque
laus et iubilatio,
salus, honor, virtus quoque
sit et benedictio:
procedenti ab utroque
compar sit laudatio.
Amen. Alleluia.

V. Panem de ccelo prestitisti
eis. [Alleluia.]
R. Omne delecta mentum in se
ha- bentem. [Alleluia.]

Divine Praises

Blessed be God.

Blessed be His Holy Name.

Blessed be Jesus Christ, true God and true man.

Blessed be the name of Jesus.

Blessed be His Most Sacred Heart.

Blessed be His Most Precious Blood.

Blessed be Jesus in the Most Holy Sacrament of the Altar.

Blessed be the Holy Spirit the Paraclete.

Blessed be the great Mother of God, Mary Most Holy.

Blessed be her holy and Immaculate Conception.

Blessed be her glorious Assumption.

Blessed be the name of Mary, Virgin and Mother.

Blessed be St. Joseph, her most chaste spouse.

Blessed be God in His Angels and in His Saints.

Amen.

Laudes Divinae

Benedictus Deus.
Benedictum Nomen Sanctum eius.
Benedictus Iesus Christus, verus Deus et verus homo.
Benedictum Nomen Iesu.
Benedictum Cor eius sacratissimum.
Benedictus Sanguis eius pretiosissimus.
Benedictus Iesus in sanctissimo altaris Sacramento.
Benedictus Sanctus Spiritus, Paraclitus.
Benedicta excelsa Mater Dei, Maria sanctissima.
Benedicta sancta eius et immaculata Conceptio.
Benedicta eius gloriosa Assumptio.
Benedictum nomen Mariae, Virginis et Matris.
Benedictus sanctus Ioseph, eius castissimus Sponsus.
Benedictus Deus in Angelis suis, et in Sanctis suis.
Amen.

Te Deum Laudamus

O God, we praise Thee: we acknowledge Thee to be the Lord.
Everlasting Father, all the earth doth worship Thee.
To Thee all the Angels, the Heavens and all the Powers,
all the Cherubim and Seraphim, unceasingly proclaim:
Holy, Holy, Holy, Lord God of Hosts!
Heaven and earth are full of the Majesty of Thy glory.
The glorious choir of the Apostles,
the wonderful company of Prophets,
the white-robed army of Martyrs, praise Thee.
Holy Church throughout the world doth acknowledge Thee:
the Father of infinite Majesty;
Thy adorable, true and only Son;
and the Holy Spirit, the Comforter.
O Christ, Thou art the King of glory!
Thou art the everlasting Son of the Father.
Thou, having taken it upon Thyself to deliver man, didst not
disdain the Virgin's womb.
Thou overcame the sting of death and hast opened to believers
the Kingdom of Heaven.
Thou sittest at the right hand of God, in the glory of the Father.
We believe that Thou shalt come to be our Judge.
We beseech Thee, therefore, to help Thy servants whom Thou
hast redeemed with Thy Precious Blood.
Make them to be numbered with Thy Saints in everlasting glory.

Te Deum Laudamus

Te Deum laudamus: te Dominum confitemur.

Te aeternum Patrem omnis terra veneratur.

Tibi omnes Angeli; tibi Caeli et universae Potestates;

Tibi Cherubim et Seraphim incessabili voce proclamant:

Sanctus, Sanctus, Sanctus, Dominus Deus Sabaoth.

Pleni sunt caeli et terra maiestatis gloriae tuae.

Te gloriosus Apostolorum chorus,

Te Prophetarum laudabilis numerus,

Te Martyrum candidatus laudat exercitus.

Te per orbem terrarum sancta confitetur Ecclesia,

Patrem immensae maiestatis:

Venerandum tuum verum et unicum Filium;

Sanctum quoque Paraclitum Spiritum.

Tu Rex gloriae, Christe.

Tu Patris sempiternus es Filius.

Tu ad liberandum suscepturus hominem, non horruisti Virginis uterum.

Tu, devicto mortis aculeo, aperuisti credentibus regna caelorum.

Tu ad dexteram Dei sedes, in gloria Patris.

Iudex crederis esse venturus.

Te ergo quaesumus, tuis famulis subveni: quos pretioso sanguine redemisti.

Aeterna fac cum sanctis tuis in gloria numerari.

V. Save Thy people, O Lord, and bless Thine inheritance!

R. Govern them, and raise them up forever.

V. Every day we thank Thee.

R. And we praise Thy Name forever, yea, forever and ever.

V. O Lord, deign to keep us from sin this day.

R. Have mercy on us, O Lord, have mercy on us.

V. Let Thy mercy, O Lord, be upon us, for we have hoped in Thee.

R. O Lord, in Thee I have hoped; let me never be put to shame.
Amen.

V. Salvum fac populum tuum, Domine, et benedic hereditati tuae.

R. Et rege eos, et extolle illos usque in aeternum.

V. Per singulos dies benedicimus te.

R. Et laudamus nomen tuum in saeculum, et in saeculum saeculi.

V. Dignare, Domine, die isto sine peccato nos custodire.

R. Miserere nostri, Domine, miserere nostri.

V. Fiat misericordia tua, Domine, super nos, quemadmodum speravimus in te.

R. In te, Domine, speravi: non confundar in aeternum.
Amen.

Come, Holy Spirit, Creator

Come, Holy Spirit, Creator blest,
and in our souls take up Thy rest;
come with Thy grace and heavenly
aid
to fill the hearts which Thou hast
made.

O comforter, to Thee we cry,
O heavenly gift of God Most High,
O fount of life and fire of love,
and sweet anointing from above.

Thou in Thy sevenfold gifts are
known;
Thou, finger of God's hand we own;
Thou, promise of the Father, Thou
Who dost the tongue with power
imbue.

Kindle our sense from above,
and make our hearts o'erflow with
love;
with patience firm and virtue high
the weakness of our flesh supply.

Veni, Creator Spiritus

Veni, Creator Spiritus,
mentes tuorum visita,
imple superna gratia
quae tu creasti pectora.

Qui diceris Paraclitus,
altissimi donum Dei,
fons vivus, ignis, caritas,
et spiritalis unctio.

Tu, septiformis munere,
digitus paternae dexterae,
Tu rite promissum Patris,
sermone ditans guttura.

Accende lumen sensibus:
infunde amorem cordibus:
infirma nostri corporis
virtute firmans perpeti.

Far from us drive the foe we dread,
and grant us Thy peace instead;
so shall we not, with Thee for guide,
turn from the path of life aside.

Oh, may Thy grace on us bestow
the Father and the Son to know;
and Thee, through endless times
confessed,
of both the eternal Spirit blest.

Now to the Father and the Son,
Who rose from death, be glory given,
with Thou, O Holy Comforter,
henceforth by all in earth and
heaven.
Amen.

Hostem repellas longius,
pacemque dones protinus:
ductore sic te praevio
vitemus omne noxium.

Per te sciamus da Patrem,
noscamus atque Filium;
Teque utriusque Spiritum
credamus omni tempore.

Deo Patri sit gloria,
et Filio, qui a mortuis
surrexit, ac Paraclito,
in saeculorum saecula.
Amen.

Come, Holy Ghost

Holy Spirit! Lord of light!
From thy clear celestial height,
Thy pure beaming radiance give

Come, thou father of the poor !
Come with treasures which endure!
Come, thou light of all that live.

Thou, of all consolers best,
Visiting the troubled breast,
Dost refreshing peace bestow;

Thou in toil art comfort sweet
Pleasant coolness in the heat;
Solace in the midst of woe.

Light immortal! light divine!
Visit thou these hearts of thine,
And our inmost being fill

If thou take thy grace away,
Nothing pure in man will stay;
All is good is turned to ill.

Veni, Sancte Spiritus

Veni, Sancte Spiritus,
et emitte caelitus
lucis tuae radium.

Veni, pater pauperum,
veni, dator munerum
veni, lumen cordium.

Consolator optime,
dulcis hospes animae,
dulce refrigerium.

In labore requies,
in aestu temperies
in fletu solatium.

O lux beatissima,
reple cordis intima
tuorum fidelium.

Sine tuo numine,
nihil est in homine,
nihil est innoxium.

Heal our wounds - our strength renew
On our dryness pour thy dew;
Wash the stains of guilt away;

Rend the stubborn heart and will;
Melt the frozen, warm the chill;
Guide the steps that go astray.

Thou, on those who evermore
Thee confess and thee adore,
In thy sevenfold gifts descend:

Give them comfort when they die;
Give them life with thee on high;
Give them joys which never end.
Amen.

Lava quod est sordidum,
riga quod est aridum,
sana quod est saucium.

Flecte quod est rigidum,
fove quod est frigidum,
rege quod est devium.

Da tuis fidelibus,
in te confidentibus,
sacrum septenarium.

Da virtutis meritum,
da salutis exitum,
da perenne gaudium,
Amen.

Hail, True Body	**Ave Verum Corpus**

Hail to thee! true Body, sprung
From the Virgin Mary's womb!
The same that on the cross was
hung,
And bore for man the bitter
doom!

Ave verum Corpus, natum
Ex Maria virgine,
Vere passum, immolatum,
In cruce pro nomine.

Thou, whose side was pierced,
and flow'd,
Both with water and with
blood;
Suffer us to taste of thee,
In our life's last agony.

Cujus latus perforatum
Vero fluxit sanguine,
Esto nobis praegustatum,
Mortis in examine.

O kind, O loving One!
O sweet Jesu, Mary's Son

O clemens, O pie,
O dulcis Jesu, Fili Mariae.

Hidden God, I Adore Thee

Godhead here in hiding, whom I do adore,
Masked by these bare shadows, shape and nothing more,
See, Lord, at your service low lies here a heart
Lost, all lost in wonder at the God you are.

Seeing, touching, tasting are in thee deceived:
How says trusty hearing? that shall be believed;
What God's Son has told me, take for truth I do;
Truth Himself speaks truly or there's nothing true.

On the cross your godhead made no sign to men,
Here your very manhood steals from human ken:
Both are my confession, both are my belief,
And I pray the prayer of the dying thief.

I am not like Thomas, wounds I cannot see,
But can plainly call you Lord and God as he;
Let me to a deeper faith daily nearer move,
Daily make me harder hope and dearer love.

You are our reminder of Christ crucified,
Living Bread, the life of us for whom he died,
Lend this life to me then: feed and feast my mind
With your sweetness that we all were meant to find.

Adoro Te Devote

Adoro deuote, latens ueritas,
te que sub his formis uere latitas.
Tibi se cor meum totum subicit,
quia te contemplans totum deficit.

Visus, tactus, gustus in te fallitur,
sed auditu solo tute creditur.
Credo quicquid dixit dei filius,
nichil ueritatis uerbo uerius.

In cruce latebat sola deitas,
sed hic latet simul et humanitas.
Ambo uere credens atque confitens,
peto quod petiuit latro penitens.

Plagas sicut Thomas non intueor,
deum tamen meum te confiteor.
Fac me tibi semper magis credere,
in te spem habere, te diligere.

O memoriale mortis domini,
panis uiuus uitam prestans homini.
Presta michi semper de te uiuere,
et te michi semper dulce sapere.

Bring the tender tale true of the Pelican;
Bathe me, Jesu Lord, in what your bosom ran
Blood whereof a single drop has power to win
All the world forgiveness of its world of sin.

Jesu, whom I look at shrouded here below,
I beseech you send me what I thirst for so,
Some day to gaze on you face to face in light
And be blest for ever with your glory's sight. Amen.

———————

Pie pellicane, Ihesu domine,
me immundum munda tuo sanguine.
Cuius una stilla saluum facere,
totum mundum posset omni scelere.

Ihesu, quem uelatum nunc aspicio,
quando fiet illud quod tam sicio?
te reuelata cernens facie,
uisu sim beatus tue glorie.

Devotions for Mass

The following section of devotions is taken from the tradition of the Church prior to the Novus Ordo mass promulgated by Pope Paul VI, which is also known as the Ordinary Form (OF) of the mass. As such, it should be noted that:

1. These are not the full set of devotions from the prior tradition, but only those that can be adapted to fit into the Ordinary Form in a way that makes sense with the way the laity participate in the celebration.
2. The faithful are called to "devout and active participation" in the mass; therefore, it is not proper for the laity to pray private prayers alongside the mass but should be actively taking part. Consequently, the following devotions should be prayed at times appropriate to unite oneself with the action of the mass and not when in conflict with other responses or prayers.
3. Due to differences in the form of the Novus Ordo from the Extraordinary Form (EF) of the mass, it may not as obvious when these prayers are to be said. Further, while many parts remain the same, they might not be widely known by their proper names. The following page helps clarify these issues.

The Introit - The opening antiphon is not part of many OF masses. In some places, it is after the opening hymn - especially with longer processions or during solemn masses where the altar is incensed. In the EF, the introit is between the Confiteor and the Kyrie.

The Confiteor - Begins "I confess to Almighty God..."

The Collect - The conclusion of the opening rites. The celebrant invites the gathered to pray and after a short silence proclaims the prayer of the day.

The Epistle - Before the Second Vatican Council there was only one reading at mass known as the Epistle. The prayer at the Epistle may be said where appropriate during the Liturgy of the Word prior to the Gospel.

The Gospel - The reading from the Gospels.

The Offertory - The bread and wine, along with gifts for support of the church and the poor are brought to the altar.

At the Offering of the Chalice - The priest raises the chalice and the people respond "Blessed be God forever," the priest then bows and prays these words. Italicized from the EF.

Washing the Fingers - The priest concludes the Offertory by washing his fingers.

The Orate Fratres - Begins "Pray, brothers and sisters..."

Prayer over the Gifts - The priest prays a secret prayer over the gifts after the Orate Fratres, prior to the Preface.

Preface - The prayer after "Lift up your hearts / We lift them up to the Lord / Let us give thanks to the Lord our God / It is right and just..."

The Oblation - Begins "Be pleased, O God, we pray, to bless, acknowledge, and approve this offering..."

Elevation of the Host - The priest raises the consecrated Host

Elevation of the Chalice - The priest shows the chalice after consecration

Breaking of the Host - The priest breaks the Host.

Puts a piece of the Host in the Chalice - The priest puts part of the Host in the Chalice.

Spiritual Communion - For if you are not going to receive communion.

The Ablution - The Eucharistic vessels are purified

After Communion - The priest will return to his chair to signify the end of Communion.

The Last Collect - The prayer after Communion.

The Blessing - Contains "May almighty God bless you, the Father, and the Son, and the Holy Spirit."

NB. There are more parts of the mass, and more prayers that can be adapted from the EF to pray along with the priest in the OF; however, it always more important to be present and participating in the prescribed way with the congregation. Even these prayers may not always be able to be said without sacrificing active participation in the OF of the mass depending on how your local mass is celebrated. In these cases, deference should *always* be given to active participation. The purpose of these prayers is to deepen and enrich the active prayer of laypersons, allowing them to *pray with the mass* rather than falling into the trap of spectating. They should never be used in a way that becomes burdensome or conflicts with the ordinary participation in the mass.

These devotions are taken from the *Gate of Heaven*, 1879.

ON GOING INTO CHURCH.

O Lord, in the multitude of thy mercies, I will enter into thy house, and praise Thy Holy Name.

AT TAKING HOLY WATER.

Purify my heart and lips, O Lord, that I may be worthy to offer up my prayers to thee

OR

Sprinkle me, O Lord, with hyssop, and I shall be cleansed : wash me, and I shall be whiter than *snow*

PRAYER REFORE MASS BEGINS.

O Divine Jesus ! Sacred Victim, offered to save mankind ! Grant that I may assist at this holy Altar with Faith, with Hope, and with the most tender Love. Amen.

A PRAYER AT THE BEGINNING OF THE MASS.

I adore thee, O my God, and I firmly believe that the Mass, at which I am going to assist, is the sacrifice of the body and blood of thy Son Christ Jesus, my Savior. Oh, grant that I may assist at it with the attention, reverence, and awe due to such a hoJy mystery and grant that, by the merits of the Victim there offered for me, I myself may become an agreeable sacrifice to thee, who lives and reigns with the same Son and Holy Ghost, one God, world without end. Amen.

AT THE INTROIT. *Chant that begins the MASS*

O my God, direct my steps, I beseech thee, in the way of thy commandments, and grant that nothing may ever separate me from thy love. Blessed are they that are undefiled in the way; that walk in the law of the Lord. Glory be to the Father, and to the Son, and to the Holy Ghost, as it was in the beginning, is now, and ever shall be, world without end.

A PRAYER AT THE CONFITEOR.

O my God, I bow down myself before thee, confessing that I have many ways offended thee in thought, word, and deed; and that I am not worthy of the many blessings thou bestow upon me. Give me grace, O God, from this time to love thee more, and to do always what is pleasing in thy sight. O blessed Virgin Mary, and all ye saints and angels, vouchsafe to intercede for me; and may the almighty and merciful Lord grant to us all pardon and peace. Amen.

A PRAYER AT THE COLLECT.

O Almighty and eternal God, we humbly beseech thee mercifully to give ear to the prayers here offered thee by thy servant in the name of thy whole Church, and in behalf of us thy people. Accept them to the honor of thy name, and the good of our souls ; and grant to us all mercy, grace, and salvation. Through our Lord Jesus Christ Amen.

A PRAYER AT THE EPISTLE.

O my God, I thank thee that thou hast called me to the knowledge of thy holy law, while so many of my fellow creatures are left in darkness and ignorance. I desire to receive with all my heart thy divine commandments, and to hear with reverence the lessons which thou address to us by the mouth of thy prophets and apostles. Give me grace, O my God, not only to know thy will, but also to do it. Amen

AT THE GOSPEL.

O Jesus ,thou hast the words of eternal life; teach me, I beseech thee, what I must do to merit and obtain that life. "If thou wilt -enter into life, keep thee commandments.
— Thou shalt love the Lord thy God with thy whole heart, and with thy whole soul, and with thy whole mind, and with thy whole strength. Seek first the kingdom of God and his justice, and all other things shall be added unto you.
— Be perfect, as your Father in heaven is perfect
— Love your neighbor as yourself.
— Love your enemies; do good to them that hate you, and pray for them that persecute you.
— If any man will come after me, let him deny himself; let him take his cross and follow me.
— Watch and pray, that you enter not into temptation.
— Happy are they who hear the word of God and keep it."

O my Savior, give me grace to lay to heart these and al thy holy precepts, and to practice them. What will it avail me to know the way of life, if I do not show forth in my conduct that I am thy disciple. O Jesus, help me to believe in thee, to love thee, and to imitate thee.

A PRAYER AT THE OFFERTORY.

Accept, O eternal Father, this offering which is here made to thee by thy minister, in the name of us all here present, and of thy whole Church. It is as yet only bread and wine, but, by a miracle of thy power and grace, will shortly become the body and blood of thy beloved Son. He is our High Priest, and he is our Victim. With him and through him we desire to approach to thee this day, and by his hands to offer thee this sacrifice, for thine own honor, praise, and glory; in thanksgiving for all thy benefits ; in satisfaction for all our sins, and for obtaining conversion for all unbelievers, and mercy, grace, and salvation for all thy faithful. And with this offering of thine only-begotten Son, we offer ourselves to thee, begging that, through this sacrifice, we may be happily united to thee, and that nothing in life or death may ever separate us any more from thee. Through Jesus Christ our Lord. Amen.

AT THE OFFERING OF THE CHALICE.

In a contrite heart and humble spirit may we be accepted by thee, O Lord; and let our sacrifice be pleasing in thy sight, O Lord God. *Come, O almighty and eternal God, the sanctifier, and bless this sacrifice prepared for thy holy name.*

A PRAYER AT THE WASHING THE FINGERS.

O most pure and holy God, wash my soul, I beseech thee, from every stain, and grant that I may be worthy to assist with a clean heart at this most holy sacrifice.

AT THE ORATE FRATRES

Receive, O Lord, this sacrifice at the hands of thy minister, to the praise and glory of thine own name, for our benefit, and that of all thy holy Church.

AT THE PRAYER OVER THE GIFTS

Mercifully hear our prayers, O Lord, and graciously accept this oblation which we thy servants make to thee; and as we offer it to the honor of thy name, so may it be to us a means of obtaining thy grace here, and life everlasting here after Through our Lord Jesus Christ.

AT THE PREFACE

Let us lift ourselves up to heaven, O my soul, and render thanks to the Lord our God. How just is it, O holy Father, and how reasonable, to glorify thee, to give thee (hanks, at all times and in all places, as our benefactor and our God. Through Jesus Christ, the angels and the virtues of the heavens, the Cherubim and Seraphim, emulate each other in celebrating thy glory and singing thy praises. May I, great God, unite my heart and voice with their celestial songs, and cry with them: Holy, holy, holy, Lord God of Sabaoth. Heaven and earth are full of thy glory. Hosanna in the highest. Blessed is he that cometh in the name of the Lord, and will shortly descend upon this altar

WHEN THE PRIEST SIGNS THE OBLATION.

Give ear, we beseech thee, O Lord, to the prayers of thy servant, who is here appointed to make this oblation in our behalf; and grand that it may obtain all those blessings which he asks

AT THE ELEVATION OF THE HOST.

Hail, Incarnate Word, sacrificed for me and all mankind! Hail, holy Victim, offered once for us upon the altar of the Cross, and still daily offered upon our altars to the end of time. I bless thee, I adore thee, I love thee. Oh, let not this sacrifice be offered for me in vain, but make me now and for ever wholly thine.

AT THE ELEVATION OF THE CHALICE.

Hail, sacred Blood, flowing from the wounds of Jesus Christ, and washing away the sins of the world ! Oh, cleanse, sanctify, and preserve my soul, " that nothing may ever separate me from thee

AT THE BREAKING OF THE HOST

Thy body was broken, and thy blood was shed for us ; grant that the commemoration of this holy mystery may obtain for us peace, and that those who receive it may find everlasting rest.

THE PRIEST PUTS PART OF THE HOST INTO THE CHALICE.

Thy body was broken, and thy blood shed for us : grant that the commemoration of thy holy mystery may obtain for us peace: and that those who receive it may find ever lasting rest. O Lord our God, pure and spotless Victim, who only can satisfy the justice of an offended God; vouchsafe to make me partaker of the merits of thy sacrifice. What lessons of humility, meekness, charity and patience do thou now give me! Impress these virtues upon my heart, that it may be to thee a pleasant habitation, wherein thou may repose, as in an abode of peace.

PRAYER FOR SPIRITUAL COMMUNION

(if not receiving the Eucharist)

Though I cannot now receive this sacrament, O most loving Jesus, 1 adore thee with a lively faith, who are present in this sacrament by virtue of thy infinite power, wisdom, and goodness. — All my hope is in thee; I love thee, O Lord, with all my heart, who hast so loved me and I desire to receive thee spiritually; come therefore, to me, O dear Lord, and fill my soul with thy presence; and 1 beseech thee to prepare my soul for that happy time when I shall be permitted to approach thy altar, and partake of the bread of life; deliver me from all sin, give me strength against my temptations, and make me always obedient to thy commands ; and let me never be separated from thee, my Savior, who, with the Father and the Holy Ghost, lives and reigns, one God, for ever and ever. Amen.

PRAYER DURING THE ABLUTION.

I adore thy goodness, O gracious Lord, in admitting me to be present, this day at that holy sacrifice, where thou art both priest and victim. Oh, make me always sensible of so great a blessing, and grant me a part in the fruits of thy death and passion.

PRAYER AFTER COMMUNION

One thing I have asked of the Lord, this will I seek after, that I may dwell in the house of the Lord all the days of my life. Taste and see that the Lord is sweet, blessed is the man, that hopes in Him.

AT THE LAST COLLECT.

Most gracious God, Father of mercy, grant, I beseech thee, that this adorable sacrifice of the blessed body and blood of thy son, our Lord Jesus Christ, may obtain for us mercy, and the remission of all our sins. Amen.

AT THE BLESSING.

I thank thee O Lord, for making me a Christian and a Catholic; pour forth thy blessing and thy grace upon me that I may serve thee with fidelity and perseverance.

PRAYER AFTER MASS.

I return thee most hearty thanks, O my God, through Jesus Christ thy Son, that thou hast been pleased to deliver him up to death for us, and to give us his body and blood, both as a sacrament and a sacrifice, in these holy mysteries, at which thou hast permitted me to assist this day. May all heaven and earth bless and praise thee for all thy mercies. Pardon me, O Lord, all thee distractions and negligences which I have been guilty of this day in thy sight; and let me not depart without thy blessing. I desire from this moment to give up myself wholly into thy hands ; and I beg that my thoughts, words, and actions may always tend to thy glory, through the same Jesus Christ our Lord. Amen

Litanies

Note that there are six litanies approved for public use by the Catholic Church. They are:

- Litany of the Holy Name of Jesus
- Litany of the Blessed Virgin Mary
- Litany of the Most Precious Blood*
- Litany of the Saints
- Litany of the Sacred Heart
- Litany of St. Joseph

All other litanies are for private and personal devotion.

*not present below

This page intentionally blank.

The Holy Name of Jesus

Lord have mercy upon us.
Lord have mercy upon us.
Christ have mercy upon us.
Christ have mercy upon us.
Lord have mercy upon us.
Lord have mercy upon us.
Christ hear us.
Christ graciously hear us.

[Respond: *Have mercy on us.*]
God the Father of heaven,
God the Son, Redeemer of the world,
God the Holy Ghost,
Holy Trinity, one God,
Jesus, Son of the living God, J
esus, Splendor of the Father,
Jesus, Brightness of eternal Light,
Jesus, King of glory,
Jesus, the Sun of justice,
Jesus, Son of the Virgin Mary,
Jesus, most admirable,
Jesus, the mighty God,
Jesus, the Father of the world to come,
Jesus, the Angel of great counsel,
Jesus, most powerful,

Jesus, most patient,

Jesus, most obedient,

Jesus, meek and humble of heart

Jesus, Lover of Chastity,

Jesus, our Beloved,

Jesus, the God of peace,

Jesus, the Author of life,

Jesus, the Example of all virtues,

Jesus, the zealous Lover of souls,

Jesus, our God,

Jesus, our Refuge,

Jesus, the Father of the poor,

Jesus, the Treasurer of the faithful,

Jesus, the Good Shepherd,

Jesus, the true Light,

Jesus, the Eternal Wisdom,

Jesus, infinite Goodness,

Jesus, our Way and our Life,

Jesus, the Joy of Angels,

Jesus, the Joy of Angels,

Jesus, the Master of the Apostles,

Jesus, the Teacher of the Evangelists,

Jesus, the Strength of Martyrs,

Jesus, the Light of Confessors,

Jesus, the Purity of Virgins,

Jesus, the Crown of all Saints,

Be merciful,
Spare us, O Jesus.
Be merciful.
Graciously hear us, O Jesus.

[Respond: *Lord Jesus, deliver us.*]
From all sin,
From thy wrath,
From the snares of the devil,
From the spirit of fornication,
From everlasting death,
From neglect of thy inspirations,
Through the mystery of thy holy Incarnation,
Through thy Nativity,
Through thy Infancy,
Through thy most divine Life,
Through thy Labors,
Through thine Agony and Passion,
Through thy Cross and Dereliction,
Through thy Weariness and Faintness,
Through thy Death and Burial,
Through thy Resurrection,
Through thine Ascension,
Through thy Joys,
Through thy glory,

Lamb of God, who takes away the sins of the world.
Spare us, O Jesus,
Lamb of God, who takes away the sins of the world,
Graciously hear us, O Jesus.
Lamb of God, who takes away the sins of the world,
Have mercy on us, O Jesus.
Jesus, hear us.
Jesus, graciously hear us.

O Lord Jesus Christ, who hast said: "Ask, and ye shall receive; seek, and ye shall find; knock, and it shall be opened unto you" grant, we beseech thee, to us who ask the gift of thy divine love, that we may love thee with our whole heart, in word and work, and never cease from showing forth thy praise.
O God, who hast appointed thine only begotten Son the Savior of mankind, and hast commanded that he should be called Jesus; mercifully grant, that we may enjoy in heaven the blessed vision of Him, whose holy Name we venerate upon earth. Through the name our Lord.
Amen.

Litany of The Blessed Virgin Mary (Litany of Loreto)

Lord, have mercy.
Lord, have mercy.
Christ have mercy.
Christ have mercy.
Lord have mercy.
Lord have mercy.
God the Father of heaven,
Have mercy on us.
God the Son, Redeemer of the world,
Have mercy on us.
God the Holy Spirit,
Have mercy on us.
Holy Trinity, one God,
Have mercy on us.

(Respond after each line: Pray for us.)
Holy Mary,
Holy Mother of God,
Holy Virgin of virgins,
Mother of Christ,
Mother of the Church,
Mother of mercy,
Mother of divine grace,
Mother of hope,

Mother most pure,
Mother most chaste,
Mother inviolate,
Mother undefiled,
Mother most amiable,
Mother most admirable,
Mother of good counsel,
Mother of our Creator,
Mother of our Savior,
Virgin most prudent,
Virgin most venerable,
Virgin most renowned,
Virgin most powerful,.
Virgin most merciful,
Virgin most faithful,
Mirror of justice,
Seat of wisdom,
Cause of our joy,
Spiritual vessel,
Vessel of honor,
Singular vessel of devotion,
Mystical rose,
Tower of David,
Tower of ivory,
House of gold,
Ark of the covenant,

Gate of heaven,

Morning star,

Health of the sick,

Refuge of sinners,

Comfort of Migrants,

Comforter of the afflicted,

Help of Christians,

Queen of Angels,

Queen of Patriarchs,

Queen of Prophets,

Queen of Apostles,

Queen of Martyrs,

Queen of Confessors,

Queen of Virgins,

Queen of all Saints,

Queen conceived without original sin,

Queen assumed into heaven,

Queen of the most holy Rosary,

Queen of Families,

Queen of Peace,

Lamb of God, you take away the sins of the world,
Spare us, O Lord.
Lamb of God, you take away the sins of the world,
Graciously hear us, O Lord.

Lamb of God, you take away the sins of the world,
Have mercy on us.

Pray for us, O holy Mother of God,
That we may be made worthy of the promises of Christ.

Let us pray,
Grant, we beseech you, Lord God, that we your servants
may rejoice in continual health of mind and body and, by
the glorious intercession of Blessed Mary, ever Virgin, may
we be delivered from present sorrow to delight in joy
eternal. Through Christ our Lord.
Amen.

Litany of the Saints

Lord have mercy.
Lord have mercy.
Christ have mercy.
Christ have mercy.
Lord have mercy.
Lord have mercy.
Christ hear us.
Christ graciously hear us
God, the Father of heaven,
Have mercy on us.
God the Son, Redeemer of the world,
Have mercy on us.
God, the Holy Spirit,
Have mercy on us.
Holy Trinity, One God,
Have mercy on us.

[Respond: *Pray for us.*]
Holy Mary,
Holy Mother of God,
Holy Virgin of virgins,
Saint Michael,
Saint Gabriel,
Saint Raphael,

All ye holy angels and archangels,

All ye holy orders of blessed spirits,

Saint John the Baptist,

Saint Joseph,

All ye holy patriarchs and prophets.

Saint Peter,

Saint Paul,

Saint Andrew,

Saint James,

Saint John,

Saint Thomas,

Saint James,

Saint Philip,

Saint Bartholomew.

Saint Matthew,

Saint Simon,

Saint Thaddeus,

Saint Matthias,

Saint Barnabas,

Saint Luke,

Saint Mark,

All ye holy apostles and evangelists,

All ye holy disciples of our Lord.

All ye holy Innocents,

Saint Stephen,

Saint Lawrence,

Saint Vincent,

Saints Fabian and Sebastian,

Saints John and Paul,

Saints Cosmas and Damian,

Saints Gervase and Protase,

All ye holy martyrs,

Saint Sylvester,

Saint Gregory,

Saint Ambrose,

Saint Augustine.

Saint Jerome,

Saint Martin,

Saint Nicolas,

All ye holy bishops and confessors,

All ye holy doctors,

Saint Anthony,

Saint Benedict,

Saint Bernard,

Saint Dominic,

Saint Francis,

All ye holy priests and levites,

All ye holy monks and hermits.

Saint Mary Magdalen,

Saint Agatha,

Saint Lucy,

Saint Agnes,
Saint Cecily,
Saint Catherine,
Saint Anastasia,
All ye holy virgins and widows,

All ye holy men and women, Saints of God,
Make intercession for us.
Be merciful,
Spare us, O Lord.
Be merciful,
Graciously hear us, O Lord.

[Respond: *O Lord, deliver us.*]
From all evil,
From all sin,
From Thy wrath,
From a sudden and unprovided death,
From the snares of the devil,
From anger, and hatred, and all ill will,
From the spirit of fornication,
From lightning and tempest,
From the scourge of earthquake.
From pestilence, famine and war,
From everlasting death,
Through the mystery of Thy holy Incarnation,
Through Thy coming,

Through Thy nativity,

Through Thy baptism and holy fasting,

Through Thy Cross and Passion,

Through Thy death and burial,

Through Thy holy Resurrection,

Through Thine admirable Ascension,

Through the coming of the Holy Spirit the Paraclete,

In the day of judgment,

[Respond: *We beseech Thee, hear us.*]

We sinners,

That Thou wouldst spare us,

That Thou wouldst pardon us,

That Thou wouldst bring us to true penance,

That Thou wouldst govern and preserve Thy holy Church,

That Thou wouldst preserve our Apostolic Prelate, and all ecclesiastical orders in holy religion,

That Thou wouldst humble the enemies of Thy holy Church,

That Thou wouldst give peace and true concord to Christian kings and princes,

That Thou wouldst grant peace and unity to all Christian people,

That Thou wouldst bring back to the unity of the Church all those who have strayed away, and lead to the light of the Gospel all unbelievers,

That Thou wouldst confirm and preserve us in Thy holy
service,
That Thou wouldst lift up our minds to heavenly desires,
That Thou wouldst render eternal blessings to all our
benefactors,
That Thou wouldst deliver our souls, and the souls of our
brethren, relations and benefactors, from eternal
damnation,
That Thou wouldst give and preserve the fruit of the earth,
That Thou wouldst give eternal rest to all the faithful
departed,
That Thou wouldst graciously hear us,
Son of God,

Lamb of God, Who takest away the sins of the world,
Spare us, O Lord.
Lamb of God, Who takest away the sins of the world,
Graciously hear us, O Lord.
Lamb of God, Who takest away the sins of the world,
Have mercy on us.
Christ hear us.
Christ, graciously hear us.
Lord, have mercy.
Christ, have mercy.
Lord, have mercy.

Our Father ...

Psalm 69

Deign, O Lord, to rescue me; O Lord, make haste to help me Let them be put to shame and confounded who seek my life. Let them be turned back in disgrace who desire my ruin. Let them retire in their shame who say to me, "Aha, aha!" But may all who seek Thee exult and be glad in Thee, And may those who love Thy salvation say ever, "God be glorified!" But I am afflicted and poor; O God, hasten to me! Thou art my help and my deliverer; O Lord, hold not back!

Glory be to the Father, and to the Son, and to the Holy Ghost. As it was in the beginning, is now, and ever shall be, world without end.

Save Thy servants.
Amen.

Litany of the Sacred Heart

Lord, have mercy
Lord, have mercy
Christ, have mercy
Christ, have mercy
Lord, have mercy
Lord, have mercy

[Respond: *Have mercy on us.*]
God our Father in heaven
God the Son, Redeemer of the world
God the Holy Spirit
Holy Trinity, one God
Heart of Jesus, Son of the eternal Father
Heart of Jesus, formed by the Holy Spirit in the womb of
the Virgin Mother
Heart of Jesus, one with the eternal Word
Heart of Jesus, infinite in majesty
Heart of Jesus, holy temple of God
Heart of Jesus, tabernacle of the Most High
Heart of Jesus, house of God and gate of heaven
Heart of Jesus, aflame with love for us
Heart of Jesus, source of justice and love
Heart of Jesus, full of goodness and love
Heart of Jesus, well-spring of all virtue

Heart of Jesus, worthy of all praise
Heart of Jesus, king and center of all hearts
Heart of Jesus, treasure-house of wisdom and knowledge
Heart of Jesus, in whom there dwells the fullness of God
Heart of Jesus, in whom the Father is well pleased
Heart of Jesus, from whose fullness we have all received
Heart of Jesus, desire of the eternal hills
Heart of Jesus, patient and full of mercy
Heart of Jesus, generous to all who turn to you
Heart of Jesus, fountain of life and holiness
Heart of Jesus, atonement for our sins
Heart of Jesus, overwhelmed with insults
Heart of Jesus, broken for our sins
Heart of Jesus, obedient even to death
Heart of Jesus, pierced by a lance
Heart of Jesus, source of all consolation
Heart of Jesus, our life and resurrection
Heart of Jesus, our peace and reconciliation
Heart of Jesus, victim of our sins
Heart of Jesus, salvation of all who trust in you
Heart of Jesus, hope of all who die in you
Heart of Jesus, delight of all the saints

Lamb of God, you take away the sins of the world
have mercy on us
Lamb of God, you take away the sins of the world
have mercy on us
Lamb of God, you take away the sins of the world
have mercy on us

Jesus, gentle and humble of heart.
Touch our hearts and make them like your own.

Let us pray.
Grant, we pray, almighty God,
that we, who glory in the Heart of your beloved Son
and recall the wonders of his love for us,
may be made worthy to receive
an overflowing measure of grace
from that fount of heavenly gifts.
Through Christ our Lord.
Amen.

Litany of the Immaculate Conception

Lord have mercy.
Lord have mercy.
Christ have mercy.
Christ have mercy.
Lord have mercy.
Lord have mercy.
Christ hear us.
Christ, graciously hear us.
God the Father, Source of all sanctity,
Have mercy on us.
God the Son, increated Sanctity,
Have mercy on us.
God the Holy Ghost, Spirit of sanctity,
Have mercy on us.
Most sacred Trinity, one God,
Have mercy on us.

[Respond: *Pray for us.*]
Holy Mary, immaculate,
Holy Virgin, by predestination immaculate,
Holy Virgin, in thy conception immaculate,
Holy Virgin, after thy conception immaculate,
 Daughter of the Father, immaculate,
Mother of the Son, immaculate,
Spouse of the Holy Ghost, immaculate,

Seat of the most holy Trinity, immaculate,

Image of the Wisdom of God, immaculate,

Dawn of the Sun of Justice, immaculate,

Living Ark of the body of Christ, immaculate,

Daughter of David, immaculate,

Guide to Jesus, immaculate,

Virgin triumphing over original sin, immaculate,

Virgin, crushing the head of the serpent, immaculate,

Queen of heaven and earth, immaculate,

Gate of the heavenly Jerusalem, immaculate,

Dispenser of graces, immaculate,

Spouse of St. Joseph, immaculate,

Star of the world, immaculate,

Impregnable tower of the Church militant, immaculate,

Rose amid thorns, immaculate,

Olive of the fields, immaculate,

Model of all perfection, immaculate,

Cause of our hope, immaculate,

Pillar of our faith, immaculate,

Source of divine love, immaculate,

Sure sign of our salvation, immaculate,

Rule of perfect obedience, immaculate,

Pattern of holy poverty, immaculate,

School of devotion, immaculate,

Abode of chaste modesty, immaculate,

Anchor of our salvation, immaculate,

Light of Angels, immaculate,

Crown of Patriarchs, immaculate,

Glory of Prophets, immaculate,

Lady and Mistress of Apostles, immaculate,

Support of Martyrs, immaculate,

Strength of Confessors, immaculate,

Diadem of Virgins, immaculate,

Splendor of all Saints, immaculate,

Sanctity of all Christians, immaculate,

Companion of devout souls, immaculate,

Joy of those who hope in thee, immaculate,

Health of the sick, immaculate,

Advocate of sinners, immaculate,

Terror of heretics, immaculate,

Protectress of all mankind, immaculate,

Patroness of those who honor thee, immaculate,

Lamb of God, who takes away the sins of the world,
Spare us, O Lord.
Lamb of God, who takes away the sins of the world,
Graciously hear us, O Lord.
Lamb of God, who takes away the sins of the world,
Have mercy on us.

V. In thy conception, O Virgin Mary, then was immaculate.
R. Pray for us to the Father, whose son Jesus, conceived of the Holy Ghost, thou did bring forth.

Let us Pray:

O Almighty and Eternal God, who didst prepare for thy Son a worthy habitation, by the immaculate conception of the blessed Virgin Mary; we beseech thee, that, as thou didst preserve her from every stain of sin, through the merits of the pre-ordained atonement of Jesus Christ, so thou wouldst grant, that we also may come without spot to thee. Through the same Jesus Christ our Lord. Amen.

Litany of the Children of Mary

Lord have mercy on us.
Christ have mercy on us.
Daughter of God the Father, elevated above all creatures, govern
Thy children.
Mother of God the Son, and our Mother, protect
Thy children.
Spouse of the Holy Ghost, obtain the sanctification of
Thy children.

[Respond: *O Mary, hear us!*]
Mother of strength, obtain for thy children the gift of perseverance and courage,
O Mother of love, obtain for thy children a true, generous, and constant love of God,
Mother, full of zeal for the glory of thy Divine Son, obtain for thy children the gift of a g lively, prudent, and enlightened zeal,
Mother, who didst preserve thyself as pure g as the lily in the midst of thorns, obtain for thy children a love of Purity which may preserve them from all sin,
Mother, who didst never lose sight of the presence of God, obtain for thy children the grace ever to remember Him, even amidst the tumults of this world,

Mother most generous, obtain for thy children patience
and resignation in all the trials of this life,

Mother, ever calm, even at the foot of the cross obtain for
thy children the spirit of peace, which may sustain us
amidst the o afflictions of life,

Mother most faithful, obtain for thy children a lively
faith that they may behold God in all his creatures,

Mother most meek and humble, obtain for thy children
the virtues of meekness and humility,

Mother, who in all thy actions sought to please thy God,
obtain for thy children purity of intention and may our
conduct prove as thy true children,

Mother, who didst despise the world and its vanities,
obtain for thy children the grace to resist its deceitful
charms,

By thy Immaculate Conception, O mother hear thy
children!

By the fervor with which thou didst offer thyself to God
at the age of three years, O mother hear thy children!

O thou who wert ever resigned to God's holy will, obtain
for thy children perfect conformity to the will of God,
O Mother, hear us!

By thy heart pierced with a sword of grief,
O Mother, hear us!

O thou who never forsake those who confide in thee,
protect us from the snares of our enemy,
O Mother, hear as!
St. Joseph, faithful guardian of Jesus and Mary,
Pray for us.
Saints Aloysius and Stanislaus, devoted servants of Mary,
Pray for us.
Lamb of God, who takes away the sins of the world,
Hear us, O Lord.
Lamb of God, who takes away the sins of the world,
Spare us, O Lord.
Lamb of God, who takes away the sins of the world.
Have mercy on us.
Jesus, hear us.
Jesus, graciously hear us.
O Mary, full of grace, look down upon and bless thy
children.

Let us Pray:
O Jesus, who from the cross did give Mary to be the Mother
of mankind, and have placed us among her privileged
children, grand that, profiting by the graces thou hast so
abundantly shed upon us, we may realize the consoling
words: "It is impossible that a true servant of Mary should
perish." We ask it, O Jesus, by the tenderness of thy divine
Heart, and the merits of thy Holy Passion.
Amen.

Litany of the Holy Angel Guardian

Lord have mercy.
Lord have mercy.
Christ have mercy.
Christ have mercy.
Lord have mercy.
Lord have mercy.
Christ hear us.
Christ graciously hear us.
God the Father of heaven,
Have mercy on us.
God the Son, Redeemer of the world,
Have mercy on us.
God the Holy Ghost,
Have mercy on us.
Holy Trinity, one God,
Have mercy on

[Respond: *Pray for us.*]
Holy Mary, Queen of Angels,
Holy Angel, my guardian,
Holy Angel, my prince,
Holy Angel, my monitor,
Holy Angel, my counsellor,
Holy Angel, my defender,
Holy Angel, my steward,

Holy Angel, my friend,
Holy Angel, my negotiator,
Holy Angel, my intercessor,
Holy Angel, my patron,
Holy Angel, my director,
Holy Angel, my ruler,
Holy Angel, my protector,
Holy Angel, my comforter,
Holy Angel, my brother,
Holy Angel, my teacher,
Holy Angel, my shepherd,
Holy Angel, my witness,
Holy Angel, my helper,
Holy Angel, my watcher.
Holy Angel, my conductor,
Holy Angel, my preserver,
Holy Angel, my instructor,
Holy Angel, my enlightener,

Lamb of God, who takes away the sins of the world,
Spare us, O Lord.
Lamb of God, who takes away the sins of the world,
Graciously hear us, O Lord.
Lamb of God, who takes away the sins of the world,
Have mercy on us.
Christ hear us,
Christ graciously hear us.

V. Pray for us, O holy Angel-guardian,

R. That we may be made worthy of the promises of Christ.

Let us pray:

Almighty, everlasting God, who, in the counsel of thy ineffable goodness, hast appointed to all the faithful, from their mother's womb, a special Angel-guardian of their body and soul; grant that I may so love and honor him whom thou hast so mercifully given me, that, protected by the bounty of thy grace, and by his assistance, I may merit to behold , with him and all the angelic host, the glory of thy countenance in the heavenly country. Who lives and reigns, world without end. Amen.

Litany of St. Joseph

Lord have mercy.
Lord have mercy.
Christ have mercy.
Christ have mercy.
Lord have mercy.
Lord have mercy.
Christ hear us.
Christ graciously hear us.
God the Father of heaven,
Have mercy on us.
God the Son, Redeemer of the world,
Have mercy on us,
God the Holy Ghost,
Have mercy on us.
Holy Trinity, one God,
Have mercy on us.

[Respond: *Pray for us.*]
Holy Mary, Spouse of Joseph,
Holy Joseph, Spouse of the Virgin Mary,
Nursing- father of Jesus,
Man according to God's own heart,
Faithful and prudent servant,
Guardian of the virginity of Mary,
Companion and solace of Mary,

Most pure in virginity.

Most profound in humility,

Most fervent in charity.

Most exalted in contemplation,

Who was declared to be a just man by the testimony of the Holy Ghost himself,

Who was enlightened above all the heavenly mysteries,

Who was the chosen minister of the counsels of the Most High,

Who was taught from above the mystery of the Incarnate Word,

Who did journey to Bethlehem with Mary thy Spouse, being great with child,

Who finding no place in the inn, did betake thyself to a stable,

Who was thought worthy to be present when Christ was born and laid in a manger,

Who did bear in thine arms the Son of God,

Who did receive the blood of Jesus at his Circumcision,

Who did present him to the Lord in the Temple, with Mary his Mother,

Who, at the warning of the Angel, did fly into Egypt with the Child and his Mother,

Who, when Herod was dead, did return with them into the land of Israel,

Who for three days, with Mary his Mother did seek sorrowing the Child Jesus, when he was last at Jerusalem,

Who, after three days, did find him with joy sitting in the midst of the Doctors,

Who had the Lord of lords subject to thee on the earth,

Who was the happy witness of his hidden life and sacred words,

Who did die in the arms of Jesus and Mary,

Whose praise is in the Gospel: The Husband of Mary, of whom was born Jesus,

Humble imitator of the Incarnate Word,

Powerful support of the Church,

Our advocate,
St. Joseph, hear its.
Our patron,
St. *Joseph, graciously hear us.*

[Respond: *St. Joseph, hear us.*]
In all our necessities, In all our distresses,
In the our of death,
Through thy most chaste espousals,
Through thy paternal care and fidelity,
Through thy love of Jesus and Marv,
Through thy labors and toils,
Through all thy virtues,
Through thy exalted honor and eternal blessedness,
Through thy faithful intercession,

We, thy clients,
Beseech thee, hear us.

[Respond: *We beseech thee, hear us.*]
That thou wouldst vouchsafe to obtain for us, from Jesus, the pardon of our sins,
That thou wouldst vouchsafe to commend us faithfully to Jesus and Mary,
That thou wouldst vouchsafe to obtain for all, both Virgins and married, the chastity belonging to their state,
That thou wouldst vouchsafe to obtain for all congregations perfect love and concord,
That thou wouldst vouchsafe to direct all rulers and prelates in the government of their subjects,
That thou wouldst vouchsafe to assist all parents in the Christian education of their children,
That thou wouldst vouchsafe to protect all those that rely upon thy patronage,
That thou wouldst vouchsafe to support, with thy paternal help, all congregations instituted under thy name and patronage,
That thou wouldst vouchsafe to visit and stand by us, with Jesus and Mary, in the last moment of our life,
That thou wouldst vouchsafe to succor, by thy prayers and intercession, all the faithful departed,
O chaste Spouse of Mary.

O faithful Nursing-father of Jesus,
Holy Joseph,

Lamb of God who takes away the sins of the world,
Spare us, O Lord.
Lamb of God, who takes away the sins of the world,
Graciously hear us, O Lord.
Lamb of God, who takes away the sins of the world,
Have mercy on us.
Christ hear us,
Christ graciously hear us.

V. Pray for us, O blessed Joseph.
R. That we may be made worthy of the promises of Christ.

Let us Pray:
O God, who didst choose St. Joseph to be the Spouse of blessed Mary ever Virgin, and to be the Guardian and Nursing father of thy beloved Son, our Lord Jesus Christ; we humbly beseech thee to grant us, through his patronage and merits, such purity of mind and body, that, being clean from every stain, and clothed with the true marriage-garment, we may, by thy great mercy, be admitted to the heavenly nuptials. Through the same Christ our Lord.
Amen.

Litany of St. Vincent de Paul

Lord have mercy.
Lord have mercy.
Christ have mercy.
Christ have mercy.
Lord have mercy.
Lord have mercy.
Christ hear us.
Christ graciously hear us.
God the Father of heaven,
Have mercy on us.
God the Son, Redeemer of the world,
Have mercy on us.
God the Holy Ghost,
Have mercy on us.
Holy Trinity, one God,
Have mercy on us.

[Respond: *Pray for us.*]
Holy Mary,
St. Vincent of Paul,
St. Vincent, who at the tenderest age didst display a wisdom most mature,
St. Vincent, who, from thy childhood, was full of piety and compassion,

St. Vincent, who, like David, from a simple shepherd became the ruler and pastor of the people of God,

St. Vincent, who in thy captivity didst preserve a perfect freedom,

St. Vincent, the just man, who lived by faith,

St. Vincent, always supported on the firm anchor of a Christian hope,

St. Vincent, always inflamed with the fire of charity,

St. Vincent, truly simple, upright, and fearing God.

St Vincent, true disciple of Jesus Christ, always meek and humble of heart.

St. Vincent, perfectly mortified in heart and mind,

St. Vincent, ever animated with the spirit of Jesus-Christ,

St, Vincent, generous maintainer of the glory of God,

St. Vincent, ever inwardly burning and ever outwardly transported, with zeal for souls,

St. Vincent, who in Christian poverty did find the precious pearl, and the rich g treasure of the Gospel,

St. Vincent, like to the Angels in thy purity,

St. Vincent, ever faithful in obedience, and ever victorious in word,

St. Vincent, from thy earliest years constantly devoted to works of charity.

St. Vincent, who didst fly with most diligent care the slightest appearance of evil,

St. Vincent, who, in all thine actions, didst aspire to the practice of the most perfect virtue,

St. Vincent, who, like a rock, remained immovable amidst the stormy sea of this world,

St Vincent, who, constant as the sun in its course, went ever onward in the paths of truest wisdom,

St. Vincent, always invincible by all the arrows of adversity,

St Vincent, as patient in suffering as thou was indulgent in forgiving,

St. Vincent, ever docile and obedient son of the Holy Romain Church, St. Vincent, who had exceeding horror of the novel ways and subtle words of heresy,

St. Vincent, destined by a special Providence to announce the Gospel to the poor,

St. Vincent, tender father and perfect model of ecclesiastics,

St. Vincent, prudent founder of the Congregation of the Mission,

St. Vincent, wise institutor of the order Sisters of Charity,

St. Vincent, always tender in compassion, and always prompt in relieving, all the necessities of the poor,

St. Vincent, equally fervent in the practice of prayer and in the ministry of the word,

St. Vincent, perfect imitator of the life and virtues of Jesus Christ,

St. Vincent, who didst persevere to the end in eschewing evil and doing good,

St. Vincent, who, as in life so in death, was most precious in the sight of God,

(St. Vincent, who by the knowledge of absolute truth, by the love of sovereign goodness, by the joys of a blessed eternity, possesses perfect happiness,
Pray for the members of the Church, and especially for the members of this brotherhood.)

Lamb of God who takes away the sins of the world,
Spare us, O Lord.
Lamb of God who takes away the sins of the world,
Graciously hear us, O Lord.
Lamb of God who takes away the sins of the world,
Have mercy on us.

V. The Lord had led the just man through right ways.
R. And showed unto him the kingdom of God.

Let us Pray:
Great God, who, by an effect of bine infinite goodness, has renewed, in our days, in the apostolic charity and humility of thy blessed servant Vincent, the spirit of thy well-beloved Son to preach the Gospel to the poor, relieve the afflicted, console the miserable, and add new luster to the ecclesiastical order; grant, we beseech thee, through his powerful intercession, that we also, being delivered from the great misery of sin, may labor to please thee by the practice of the same humility. Through Jesus Christ our Lord.
Amen.

Litany of St. Aloysius

Lord have mercy.
Lord have mercy.
Christ have mercy.
Christ have mercy.
Lord have mercy.
Lord have mercy.
Christ hear us.
Christ graciously hear us.
God the Father of heaven,
Have mercy on us.
God the Son, Redeemer of the world,
Have mercy on us.
God the Holy Ghost,
Have mercy on us.
Holy Trinity, one God,
Have mercy on us.

[Respond: *Pray for us.*]
Holy Mary,
Holy Mother of God,
Holy Virgin of Virgins,
St. Aloysius,
Most beloved of Christ,
The delight of the Blessed Virgin,
Most chaste youth,

Angelic youth,

Most humble youth,

Model of young students,

Despiser of riches,

Enemy of vanities,

Scorner of honors,

Honor of princes

Jewel of the nobility,

Flower of innocence,

Ornament of a religious state,

Mirror of mortification,

Mirror of perfect obedience,

Lover of evangelical poverty,

Most affectionately devout,

Most zealous observer of rules,

Most desirous of the salvation of souls,

Perpetual adorer of the holy Eucharist,

Particular client of St. Ignatius,

[Respond: *Be merciful, hear us, O Lord*.]

Be merciful spare us, O Lord.

From the concupiscence of the eyes,

From the concupiscence of the flesh,

From the pride of life,

Through the merits and intercession of Aloysius,

Through his angelical purity,

Through his sanctity and glory,

We sinners,
Beseech thee hear us.

Lamb of God, who takes away the sins of the world,
Spare us O Lord.
Lamb of God, who takes away the sins of the world,
Hear us, O Lord.
Lamb of God, who takes away the sins of the world,
Have mercy on us.
Christ, hear us.
Christ, graciously hear us.

V. Pray for us, St. Aloysius.
R. That we may be made worthy of the promises of Christ.

Let us Pray.
O God! the distributor of heavenly gifts, who did unite in the angelic youth Aloysius, wonderful innocence of life with an equal severity of penance, grant through his merits and prayers that we, who have not followed the example of his innocence, may imitate his practice of penance; through our Lord Jesus Christ.
Amen.

Litany for Children

Lord have mercy on us.
Lord have mercy on us.
Christ have mercy on us.
Christ have mercy on us.
Lord have mercy on us.
Lord have mercy on us.

[Respond: *Have mercy on us.*]
Lord have mercy on us.
Jesus, almighty God,
Jesus, God of peace,
Jesus, lover of mankind,
Jesus, model of meekness and humility,
Jesus, model of innocence and simplicity,
Jesus, model of truth and sincerity,
Jesus, model of chastity and purity of heart,
Jesus, pattern of submission and obedience,
Jesus, pattern of mildness and gentleness,
Jesus, pattern of charity and goodwill to men,
Jesus, pattern of all virtues,

Be merciful, O Jesus, and spare us.
Be merciful, O Jesus, and hear us.

[Respond: *Lord Jesus, deliver us*.]

From all irreligion,

From profane ridicule and contempt of what is holy,

From the neglect of what we know to be our duty,

From carelessness in our devotions, From the neglect of thy calls and inspirations,

From lying, deceit, and hypocrisy,

From disobedience to our parents and superiors,

From stubbornness and obstinacy,

From ingratitude to those who do us good,

From all hatred and ill-will,

From seeking revenge,

From a heedless and unthinking life,

From too great a love of ourselves and our own wills,

From inattention to learning and the instructions of our superiors,

From all loss of the valuable time of youth,

We sinners,
beseech thee, hear us.

[Respond: *We beseech thee, hear us.*]

That we may love thee above all things and our neighbor as ourselves,

That our love of thee may show itself in the observance of thy commandments,

That the love of our neighbor may appear in always doing to him as we wish him to do to us,

That we may be grateful to thee, the giver of all good gifts,

That we may live soberly, justly, and godly and keep our thoughts free from all the defilement of sin,

That our thoughts, words, and actions, may be directed to thee, who art the author of life here, and happiness hereafter,

That we may make a good use of our advantages, by seeking instruction, loving our & prayers, our learning, and all other duties,

That we may hate idleness, as the source of much wickedness,

That the spirit of mildness and gentleness may appear in all our actions,

That we may bear with others' failings, as we wish them to bear with our own,

That we may live together as brothers, children of the same Father, and looking for the blessed hope, and coming of thee, our Lord and Savior Jesus Christ,

Lamb of God, who takes away the sins of the world,
Spare us, O Lord Jesus.
Lamb of God, who takes away the sins of the world,
Hear us, O Lord Jesus.
Lamb of God, who takes away the sins of the world,
Have mercy on us, O Lord Jesus.

Christ Jesus, hear us.
Christ Jesus, graciously hear us.

Let us Pray:

O Jesus, our merciful Redeemer, who did call children to thee, did embrace them, and give them thy blessing, give thy blessing to us also, we beseech thee, this day, and through the course of our lives. Grant that we may ever love thee above all things, and with our whole hearts; that we may love our neighbor as ourselves, and ardently aspire after that happiness for which we were created. Bless our parents, teachers relations, and benefactors: preserve them from evil, and direct them to all good; and grant that we may all meet together in thy eternal kingdom.

Amen.

The Seven Penitential Psalms

The penitential psalms are traditionally regarded as David's lamentations for his sins. Their designation as "penitential" goes back to the seventh century, and Pope Innocent III designated for them to be prayed during Lent. There are five primary characteristics of these psalms: 1.) sorrow for sin; 2.) desire for repentance; 3.) removing the source of sin; 4.) trust in God's goodness; 5.) gratitude for God's and mercy.

When prayed in penitence, one kneels, begins and ends with an antiphon, and says a Glory Be between each one.

ANTHEM. Remember not, O Lord, our offences, nor those of our parents, and take not revenge on our sins.

Psalm 6. — Domine, ne in furore.

I. David, in deep affliction, prays for a mitigation of the divine anger ; 4. in consideration of God's mercy : 5. His glory ; 6. his own repentance ; 8. by faith triumphs over his enemies.

O Lord, rebuke me not in thy indignation, nor chastise me in Thy wrath.

Have mercy on me, O Lord, for 1 am weak: heal me, O Lord, for my bones are troubled.

And my soul is troubled exceedingly: but Thou, O Lord, how long ?

Turn to me, O Lord, and deliver my soul: O save me for Thy mercy's sake.

For there is no one in death that is mindful of Thee and who shall confess to Thee in hell?

I have labored in my groanings, every night I will wash my bed, I will water my couch with my tears.

My eye is troubled through indignation: I have grown old among all my enemies.

Depart from me, all ye workers of iniquity: for the Lord hath heard the voice of my weeping.

The Lord hath heard my supplication: the Lord hath received my prayer.

Let my enemies be ashamed, and be very much troubled: let them be turned back, and be ashamed very speedily.

Glory be...

Psalm 31. — Beati quorum.

4. Blessings of remission of sins ; 3. misery of impenitence ; 6. confession of sins brings ease, 8. safety ; 14. joy.

Blessed are thy whose iniquities are forgiven, and whose sins are covered.

Blessed is the man to whom the Lord bath not imputed sin, and in whose spirit there is no guile.

Because I was silent, my bones grew old; whilst I cried out all the day long.

For day and night Thy hand was heavy upon me: I am turned in my anguish, whilst the thorn is fastened.

I have acknowledged my sin to Thee; and my injustice I have not concealed.

I said I will confess against myself my injustice to the Lord, and Thou hast forgiven the wickedness of my sin.

For this shall every one that is holy pray to Thee, in a seasonable time.

And yet in a flood of many waters, they shall not come nigh unto Him.

Thou art my refuge from the trouble which hath encompassed me; my joy, deliver me from them that surround me.

I will give thee understanding, and I will instruct thee in the way in which thou shalt go; I will fix my eyes upon thee.

Do not become like the horse and the mule that have no understanding.

With bit and bridle bind fast their jaws who come not near unto thee.

Many are the scourges of the sinner, but mercy shall encompass him that hopes in the Lord.

Be glad in the Lord, and rejoice ye just, and glory, all ye right of heart.

Glory be...

Psalm 37. — Domine, ne in furore.

1. David's extreme anguish ; 15. he hopes in God ; 18. his resignation , grief; 22. fervent prayer.

Rebuke me not, O Lord, in Thy indignation, nor chastise me in Thy wrath.

For Thy arrows are fastened in me ; and Thy hand hath been strong upon me.

There is no health in my flesh, because of Thy wrath ; there is no peace for my bones, because of my sins.

For my iniquities are gone over my head; and as a heavy burden are become heavy upon me.

My sores are putrefied and corrupted, because of my foolishness.

I am become miserable, and am bowed down even to the end; I walked sorrowful all the day long.

For my loins are filled with illusions; and there is no health in my flesh.

I am afflicted and bumbled exceedingly; I roared with the groaning of my heart.

Lord, all my desire is before Thee; and my groaning is not hid from thee.

My heart is troubled, my strength hath left me, and the light of my eyes itself is not with me.

My friends and my neighbors have drawn near, and stood against me.

And they that were near me stood afar off; and they that sought my soul used violence.

And they that sought evils to me spoke vain things, and studied deceits all the day long.

But I, as a deaf man, heard not; and as a dumb man not opening his mouth.

And I became as a man that hears not; and that hath no reproofs in his mouth.

For in thee, O Lord, have I hoped ; Thou wilt hear me, O Lord, my God.

For I said, Lest at any time my enemies rejoice over me; and whilst my feet are moved, they speak great things against me.

For I am ready for scourges; and my sorrow is continually before me.

For I will declare my iniquity; and I will think for my sin.

But my enemies live, and are stronger than I; and they that hate me wrongfully are multiplied.

They that render evil for good, have detracted me, because I followed goodness.

Forsake me not, O Lord my God; do no Thou depart from me.

Attend unto my help, O Lord, the God of my salvation.

Glory be...

Psalm 50. — Miserere.

1. David prays for remission of his sins; 8. for perfect sanctity ; 17. God delights not in sacrifice, but a contrite heart; 19. he prays for the building of a temple in Jerusalem, figuratively, the exaltation of the Church.

Have mercy on me, O God, according to thy great mercy.

And according to the multitude of Thy tender mercies, blot out my iniquity.

Wash me yet more from my iniquity, and cleanse me from my sin.

For I know my iniquity, and my sin is always before me.

To Thee only have I sinned, and have done evil before Thee; that Thou mayest be justified in Thy words, and mayest overcome when Thou art judged.

For behold I was conceived in iniquities; and in sins did my mother conceive me.

For behold Thou hast loved truth; the uncertain and hidden things of Thy wisdom Thou hast made manifest to me.

Thou shalt sprinkle me with hyssop, and I shall be cleansed; Thou shalt wash me, and I shall be made whiter than snow.

To my hearing Thou shalt give joy and gladness: and the bones that have been humbled shall rejoice.

Turn away Thy face from my sins, and blot out all my iniquities.

Create a clean heart in me, O God, and renew a right spirit within my bowels.

Cast me not away from Thy face; and take not Thy Holy spirit from me.

Restore unto me the joy of Thy salvation, and strengthen me with a perfect spirit.

I will teach the unjust Thy ways; and the wicked shall be converted to Thee.

Deliver me from blood, O God, Thou God of my salvation; and my tongue shall extol Thy justice.

O Lord, Thou wilt open my lips; and my mouth shall declare Thy praise.

For if Thou had desired sacrifice, I would indeed have given it; with burnt-offerings

Thou wilt not be delighted. A sacrifice to God is an afflicted spirit ; a contrite and humble heart, O God, Thou wilt not despise.

Deal favorably, O Lord, in Thy good will with Zion; that the walls of Jerusalem may be built up.

Then shalt Thou accept the sacrifice of justice, oblations, and whole burnt-offerings, then shall they lay calves upon Thy altar.

Glory be...

Psalm 101 — Domine, exaudi.

1. The extreme affliction of the Psalmist; 12. the eternity and mercy of God; 19. to be recorded, and praised by future generations; 26. the unchangeableness of God.

Hear, O Lord, my prayer, and let my cry come to Thee.

Turn not away Thy face from me; in the day when I am troubled, incline Thine ear to me.

In what day so-ever I shall call upon Thee, hear me speedily.

For my das are vanished like smoke; and my bones are grown dry like fuel for the fire.

I am smitten as grass, and my heart is withered; because I forgot to eat my bread.

Through the voice of my groaning my bone hath cleaved to my flesh.

I am become like to a pelican of the wilderness; I am like a night-raven in the house.

I have watched, and am become as a sparrow, all alone on the house-top.

All the day long my enemies reproach me; and they that praised me did swear against me.

For I did eat ashes like bread; and mingled my drink with weeping.

Because of Thy anger and indignation; for having lifted me up Thou hast thrown me down.

My days have declined like a shadow; and I am withered like grass.

But Thou, O Lord, endure for ever; and Thy memorial to all generations.

Thou shalt arise and have mercy on Zion, for it is time to have mercy on it, for the time is come.

For the stones thereof have pleased Thy servants, and they shall have pity on the earth thereof.

And the Gentiles shall fear Thy name, O Lord, and all the kings of the earth Thy glory.

For the Lord hath built up Zion; and He shall be seen in His glory.

He hath had regard to the prayer of the humble, and He hath not despised their petition.

Let these things be written unto another generation; and the people, that shall be created, shall praise the Lord.

Because He. hath looked forth from His high sanctuary; from heaven the Lord hath looked upon the earth.

That He might hear the groans of them that are in fetters; that He might release the children of the slain.

That they may declare the name of the Lord in Sion, and His praise in Jerusalem.

When the people assembled together, and kings to serve the Lord.

He answered Him in the way of his strength: Declare unto me the fewness of my days.

Call me not away in the midst of my days: Thy years are unto generation and generation.

In the beginning, O Lord, Thou Roundest the earth; and the heavens are the works of Thy hands.

They shall perish, but Thou remainest: and all of them shall grow old like a garment.

And as a vesture Thou shall change them, and they shall be changed; but Thou art always the self-same, and Thy years shall not fail.

The children of Thy servants shall continue: and their seed shall be directed for ever.

Glory be...

Psalm 129.— De profundis.

An excellent model for sinners imploring the divine mercy.

Out of the depths I have cried to thee, O Lord; Lord, hear my voice.

Let Thy ears be attentive to the voice of my supplication.

If Thou, O Lord, wilt mark iniquities, Lord, who shall stand it!

For with Thee there is merciful forgiveness: and by reason of Thy law I have waited for Thee, O Lord.

My soul hath relied on His word; my soul hath hoped in the Lord.

From the morning watch even until night, let Israel hope in the Lord.

Because with the Lord there is mercy, and with Him plentiful redemption.

And He shall redeem Israel from all his iniquities.

Glory be...

Psalm 142 —Domine, exaudi.

1. David praveth for favor in judgment; 3. re- 5resents his distress; 7. He prayeth for grace; . for deliverance ; 10, for sanctification ; 12. victory over his enemies.

Hear, O Lord, my prayer; give ear to my supplication in Thy truth; hear me in Thy justice.

And enter not into judgment with Thy servant; for in Thy sight no man living shall be justified.

For the enemy hath persecuted my soul: he hath brought down my life to the earth.

He hath made me to dwell in darkness, as those that have been dead of old; and my spirit is in anguish within me! my heart within me is troubled.

I remembered the days of old, I mediated on all Thy works: I mused upon the works of Thy hands.

I stretched forth my hands to Thee: my soul is as earth without water unto thee.

Hear me speedily, O Lord; my spirit hath fainted away.

Turn not away Thy face from me, lest I be like unto them that go down into the pit.

Cause me to hear Thy mercy in the morning; for in Thee have I hoped.

Make the way known to me wherein I should walk; for I have lifted up my soul to Thee.

Deliver me from my enemies, O Lord, to Thee have I fled; teach me to do Thy will, for Thou art my God.

Thy good spirit shall lead me into the right land; for thy name's sake, O Lord, Thou wilt quicken me in Thy justice.

Thou wilt bring my soul out of troubles: and in Thy mercy Thou wilt destroy my enemies.

And Thou wilt cut off all them that afflict my soul: for I am Thy servant.

Glory be...

ANTHEM: Remember not, O Lord, our offences, nor those of our parents; and take not revenge on our sins.

Appendix: Pronunciation of Church Latin

Vowels:

- a - *ah*, as in f*a*ther
- e - *eh*, as in *e*lm, *e*gg
- i - *ee*, as in stud*i*o, aud*i*ence, mach*i*ne
- o - *oh*, as in ph*o*ne, h*o*me
- u - *oo*, as in r*u*le, m*u*le
- y - *ee,* the same as i above

When two vowels appear together, both are pronounced except for certain diphthongs, below:

Diphthongs:

- *ae* and *oe* - pronounced like *e* above: *eh*, as in *e*lm, *e*gg
- *au* and *eu* - pronounce each vowel distinctly but said as a single syllable

Consonants:

- *b, d, f, k, l, m, n, p, s, t, v* - pronounced as in English
- *c* before an *e, i, y, ae, oe* - pronounced as *ch*
- *cc* before an *e, i, y, ae, oe* - pronounced as *t'ch*
- *ch* - pronounced as *k*
- *g* before an *e, i, y, ae, or* - pronounced soft as in *g*em
- *g* in other instances is pronounced hard as in *g*un
- *gn* - pronounced *ny*, think of the Italian food *gn*occhi
- *h* is mute except between vowels where it is pronounced *kh*
- *j* - pronounced as *y*; e.g., *J*esu (yeh-soo)
- *r* - pronounced with a light roll
- *sc* before *e, i, y, ae, or* - pronounced as *sh*
- *th* - *t,* as though no *h*, e.g., *Th*omas
- *ti* before vowels and after any latter excluding *s, t,* or *x* - *tsee*
- *x* - *ks*, as in e*x*it
- *xc* before *e, r, y, ae, oe* - pronounced as *ksh*

Acknowledgments

The following public domain texts were used in composing this book:

Gate Of Heaven: Way Of The Child Of Mary. Turnhout, Brepols & Dierckx, 1879.

The Holy Bible in English, Douay-Rheims American Edition of 1899. Translated by English College, Douai. 1899.

Little Manual Of The Sacred Heart. New York: J. Schaefer, 1887.

Missale Romanum. USA: Benziger Brothers, Inc., 1962.

Text from the Latin Vulgate version of the bible courtesy of The Clementine Text Project.

Made in the USA
Middletown, DE
20 July 2023

35494730R00080